"Knowing Sandy's heart for the Lord, her new book proved to be all I hoped it would be. *Called to Rebellion* is a scripturally grounded, prayerfully written plea to the Christian woman to recognize that, in the eyes of God, she is both a Cinderella and a Joan of Arc. It's an impassioned invitation to come and bask in the grace of Jesus Christ, and then to go and fulfill His call to impact the world—forgiven, healed, obedient, and triumphant over every ploy of the enemy of our souls."

Ron Mehl
Pastor and author of *The Ten(der) Commandments*

"*Called to Rebellion* is provoking and compassionate. Sandy Snavely is a refreshing new writer who powerfully motivates women to action and at the same time gently touches hearts. This book is a treasure for every woman who longs to find her way back to an extraordinary love for Christ."

Alice Gray
Editor of bestselling Stories for the Heart series

"God has given us a wake-up call in *Called to Rebellion*. He wants us to know our true condition and to give us the opportunity to do something about it! Let's unite in Christ and be rebels together!"

Susan Kimes
Founder and Executive Director, Chosen Women

"I must admit my first instinct was to 'rebel' against the title. But upon closer inspection, I discovered to judge this book by its cover would be to miss the rich fare that's being served inside. *Called to Rebellion* is food for the soul that will heal you as it fills you with liberating truth served up in a way that makes it go down easy."

Michelle McKinney Hammond
Author of *Secrets of an Irresistible Woman* and *What to Do Until Love Finds You*

"Sandy Snavely has a heart for God and a desire to honor the Lord in all she says and does. Her commitment to the Lord and His Word is obvious, and the message she communicates in this book is much needed. May the Lord use it for His glory."

David Hocking

HOPE for TODAY Ministries

CALLED TO REBELLION

The Key to a

Single-Hearted

Love for Christ

Sandy Snavely

Multnomah® Publishers *Sisters, Oregon*

CALLED TO REBELLION
published by Multnomah Publishers, Inc.
© 1999 by Sandy Snavely

International Standard Book Number: 1-57673-419-6

Cover by Margaret Spengler

Scripture quotations are from: *The Holy Bible,* New International Version (NIV)
©1973, 1984 by International Bible Society, used by permission of
Zondervan Publishing House
Also quoted: *The Holy Bible,* King James Version (KJV)
The Message © 1993 by Eugene H. Peterson
New American Standard Bible (NASB) © 1960, 1977
by the Lockman Foundation
The New Testament in Modern English, Revised Edition (Phillips)
© 1972 by J. B. Phillips

Multnomah is a trademark of Multnomah Publishers and is registered in the
U.S. Patent and Trademark Office.
The colophon is a trademark of Multnomah Publishers, Inc.

Printed in the United States of America

MULTNOMAH PUBLISHERS, INC.•POST OFFICE BOX 1720•SISTERS, OREGON 97759
Library of Congress Cataloging–in–Publication Data
Snavely, Sandy.
Called to rebellion: the key to single-hearted love for Christ/by Sandy
Sanvely. p.cm. Includes bibliographical references.
ISBN 1-57673-419-6 (alk. paper) 1. Christian women—Religious life.
I. Title. BV4527.S634 1999 99-24177 248.8'43–dc21 CIP

99 00 01 02 03 04 05 06 — 10 9 8 7 6 5 4 3 2 1

To my husband, Bud:

Whether I've surprised you with your favorite meal,
Or made you laugh out loud,
Or finished an impossible task:
The smile on your face is my applause.

Contents

Acknowledgments

*C*alled to Rebellion is a work from God's heart expressed through my heart and brought to completion because of the loving help and support of the many whom He has chosen to be my friends. My special thanks go first to three people who began this venture with me and who would not accept the word *defeat*. Thanks to: Bunny Wilson, my precious sister in Christ who shares my burden for God's women to come back to the heart of the Master. To my dear friend Alice Gray for her tender-hearted love and encouragement and her ability to dream great dreams for the kingdom. And also to Chip MacGregor whose confidence in my work sometimes left him out on a limb but never out of hope that this book would one day be published.

I owe a special debt of gratitude to Larry Gadbaugh, my pastor and friend, whose love for the Scriptures challenges me to think deeper. I am humbled by the kindness expressed through those who put their seal of approval on my work. To Bunny Wilson, Alice Gray, Susan Kimes, Michelle McKinney, and Ron Mehl, thank you for your gracious endorsements.

Loving thanks also to the many incredible friends who encouraged and prayed fervently for me as I wrote and rewrote—Connie McClellan, Maria Fitz, Sandi Day, Susan Neely, Myrna Alexander, Lori Blair, Mary Starrett, and my prayer partners in the two prayer groups of which I am a participant. To Nancy Cole for motivating me to be a part of the 2 percent of people who accomplish their goals and to the leadership and friends at Grace Community Church for being a true reflection of Christ's heart to me.

I offer my humble gratitude to the family of Multnomah Publishers for their integrity and commitment to biblical truth. A large thanks to Nancy Thompson, my noteworthy editor, for being tough, tender, and talented and for taking me beyond where I thought I could go as a new writer. Thanks also to Matt Jacobson for asking to see this manuscript and for his courage to stand by the title.

And a personal note to my family—thank you for being my mirror. To my husband and captain, Bud—praises to you for sharing my heart for this project and for your brilliant computer skills that kept my words from getting lost in space. You make my life as your wife both meaningful and fun. To my children Annette Fletcher and Dean Snavely, thank you for all the memories you have given me that have tenderized my heart and sharpened my character. To my treasured sister and friend, Rosanne Larson and to my brother, Kenny Amundsen —thanks for your life-long enthusiasm and encouragement. And to my mom, dad, and mother-in-law who see from heaven and rejoice—love and hugs will come soon and very soon.

And to the many other friends who prayed—thank you. You are *all* rebels in your own right—fearless followers of Christ and resisters of the Impostor's invitation to mediocrity.

My heart overflows with a good theme; I address my verses to the King; My tongue is the pen of a ready writer.

PSALM 45:1, NASB

Foreword

*I*t was just another radio interview, or so I thought. While waiting for the music to come on signaling we were on the air, I paused to admire the neatly groomed, blond, mature woman who would be my host. She had a disarming smile and yet something about her demeanor was no-nonsense. It was during the interview that my desire to become lifelong friends with Sandy developed.

Years later, I discovered that our interview was one of the first she had done. This revelation was stunning because I thought Sandy was one of the most outstanding radio talk show hosts I had ever heard. Her direct yet compassionate, informed yet humble manner endeared her to the listening audience and those she interviewed. I was amazed at the lively, call-in participation from so many of all races, ages, genders.

Now Sandy meets us on the written page with *Called to Rebellion*. This is a piece that will provoke us to shake off complacency, elevate us to a higher spiritual level and position us to rise up and respond against the deception, lies, and confusion prevalent in today's society.

Our common passion for seeing the hearts of women turned to God is what bonded us together. Coming from an atheistic background, when I fell in love with Jesus, I also thirsted for His Word. One day I ran across a Scripture that said, "Wives, submit yourself unto your own husband as unto the Lord." My first thought was, *Why would God mess up a good book with a Scripture verse like that?* But it was my desire to serve Christ that motivated me to pursue His purpose in that area. God was faithful to teach me that submission is a very powerful, positive, and aggressive principle designed for every man and woman whether single or married. It set me free, and I authored and coauthored books titled *Liberated through Submission* and *The Master's Degree—Majoring in your Marriage.*

In like manner, Sandy pursues the truth on many controversial subjects and does it with the skill of a master surgeon. No longer do we have to buy what the world is selling or surrender to what appears to be general consensus. We have been called, not to be passive, but assertive in our lifestyle and in the teaching of our children. Our commission is to be holy and set apart so that "our light may shine" and sinners may be saved. It is thrilling to now have a companion book that proclaims truth in a practical, yet stimulating way.

Every Christian woman needs this book—singles to prepare one day for marriage and family, married women who want to walk in faith and power. You will laugh and cry, repent and be renewed. And just like me, you are sure to fall in love with the author, Sandy Snavely.

Bunny Wilson

I hate the word submission." Being in a Bible study with Patty was like roller skating through a minefield. *"I have a right to my own ideas. I don't care what Peter or Paul or any other old fuddy-duddy has to say about it. They were just a bunch of insecure, dominating men!"*

Following a heated business meeting, Ruth declared with subversive resolve, *"I will answer to no one. If they push me too far they will find out just how much power I really have."*

The coffee cups rattled as Edith pounded her fist on the kitchen table, *"I helped build this church, and if that upstart of a pastor thinks for one minute he can change the way we do things here, he has another think coming."*

Stacey tightened her grip on the steering wheel as she replayed the argument she had with her parents, *"What kind of Christians are they anyway? Until they straighten out their own lives, I will not allow them to run mine."*

Jean explained her enlightened insight into Christianity. *"I love the Bible, but I just have a problem with using terms like 'sinner' and 'born again.' I think the world is judgmental enough without inflicting guilt on everyone."*

Ah, sweet rebellion! Declarations of independence flowing from the lips of God's women are but a sampling of the spoils from Satan's war with God. They are nostalgic reminders of that defining moment, before the creation of man, when he raised his fist before the hosts of heaven and shouted, *I shall be like God. Look at me. I am lovely and powerful. I have plans, and dreams … Oh yes, I have great dreams! Do you love this kingdom of the Master? I tell you, it is a pitiful wrinkle on the parchment of my design. Come with me, you angels. Do you see how He has treated me? I have been ordered out of heaven simply because I had the courage to say what I think. He has called my independence* rebellion… *I call it* freedom!

Lucifer was the most beautiful of all God's angels. Yet for his longing for omnipotence, he turned his back against his Creator. Is it possible that this brilliant angelic being was ignorant of the consequences that were to follow his intentional rebellion? Until Lucifer contended with God, all heaven was innocent of wrath's true meaning. Yet the moment those words of independence rolled off Satan's lips, a flash of lightening split the sky and set fire to his new address. The angels who chose to follow him enlisted in his army of demons. A counter kingdom with a counterfeit ruler was established. Their mission was clearly defined by their commander: to destroy the kingdom of God and to set up a new kingdom—

a kingdom where there would be no rules, no limits, and no principles that would restrict the vulgar impulses of their leader's twisted heart.

There is a reason why the title *Called to Rebellion* may have captured your attention. Perhaps you are one who treasures your independence. Or maybe the word *rebellion* secretly makes your heart flutter with a sense of seductive intrigue. You might be a woman who loves the thrill of flirting with danger—stretching obedience to the limit to see how flexible the love of God really is. Or, quite possibly, this book is in your hands because you are rightfully suspicious that the message behind the title is a flagrant invitation to lead women away from biblical truth. Despite your reasons for reading this book, if your heart's desire is to have a single-hearted love for Christ, you and I have much in common.

ROOTS OF REBELLION

Is it possible for a holy God to call His people to rebellion? If you trace the word *rebellion* throughout the Scriptures you will find a none-to-flattering account of how fickle the hearts of God's children have been. The temptation to rebel against our Creator has been the plague of mankind since the incident in the Garden when Eve succumbed to the question posed by the serpent, *"Indeed, has God said, 'You shall not eat from any tree of the Garden'"*?

Something else took place under the forbidden tree that I believe makes the case for rebellion not only reasonable but also necessary. When Eve turned her attention toward the serpent she turned her focus away from God. When Eve listened to the voice of the serpent as he challenged her Master's words she turned her ears away from God. When Eve bit into the forbidden fruit she turned her back on God. When all was said and done, Eve became the first to prove how sin distracts, deceives, and destroys the human heart.

> Let no man say when he is tempted, I am tempted of God: for God cannot be tempted with evil, neither tempteth he any man: But every man is tempted, when he is drawn away of his own lust, and enticed. Then when lust hath conceived, it bringeth forth sin: and sin, when it is finished, bringeth forth death. (James 1:13–15, KJV)

The Master is our rightful ruler. He has the right to rule over us because He created us and He loves us with flawless affection. The Impostor is the insurrectionist whose chief aim is to unseat the Master from His throne. We are the prey who often fall for the Impostor's lies, and like Eve in the Garden, we turn our backs on our God. God calls this *rebellion* but the Impostor calls it *allegiance* because when our backs are turned against the Master, our faces are turned toward the Imposter. God's call to us is to rebel *against* the Impostor so that we can love Him with single-hearted devotion.

When I invited Jesus to be the Lord over my life, I had every intention of following His ways forever. That didn't happen. The reasons for my struggle were many. At the top of the list was my failure to understand that before I became a Christian I had been a servant of the enemy of God. Because Satan was such a subtle leader, I was unaware of how discretely he had been directing my life since childhood. His personality also was such a mystery to me that I wouldn't have recognized how similar my character traits were to his.

I was angry, independent, prideful, selfish, and I had become quite a convincing liar. I knew these things were wrong but I didn't know just how wrong they were. My sin habits had the fingerprints of Satan all over them.

Second, each time I was faced with areas in my life that needed altering I would go to my heavenly Father and beg Him to help me to stop doing those things which were counter to His will. Then, after a short time of successful restraint, I would fall right back into the same sinful patterns I had promised never to do again. What I failed to understand was what it meant to truly repent. I thought I could just tell God how sorry I was for the things I had done, promise to never do them again, ask Him to help me do better, and God would zap me with His magic wand and make me a new woman. But God doesn't work that way. Instead, I discovered that being sorry for sin and repenting of sin are two different things. To be sorry means to have a momentary brush with regret. To repent means to accept God's view of sin, to agree with Him regarding its destructive consequences, and to fully, willingly, wholeheartedly let go of my love for it.

And third, I failed to see who I was pledging my allegiance to each time I knowingly fell back into my old ways of living. Each time I shouted at my husband, each time I told a little lie to cover a mistake, each time I stamped my foot because life wasn't going my way, I was unwittingly sitting by the forbidden tree conversing with the enemy. *Did God really say you shouldn't do that? Are you sure what you did was really sin? Surely God doesn't want you to be a doormat to someone who is so obviously wrong.* My rebellion against the Master was allegiance to the Impostor.

I can never be truly aligned with the will of the Master

until I am willing to put away all those behaviors that were a part of my old life. When I am willing to agree with God and call my wrong behavior by its rightful name—*sin*—Satan will lose his ability to lure me back into his domain. I cannot serve two masters.

WHERE IS THE LIGHT?

Christianity demands a life that has been radically changed. The shadow of the cross ought to stretch across every area of our lives if we are to be believed for what we believe. Instead, passionate Christianity, the kind that should shine like a floodlight in the dark, looks today more like a matchstick in the rain. While the world denounces Christianity as being irrelevant for this modern age, present-day Christianity provides little evidence for a convincing rebuttal.

The statistics prove this to be shamefully true.
- 50% of Christian marriages end in divorce
- 81% of Americans say they are Christians, while only 37% of Americans take the Bible seriously
- 43% of Evangelicals believe Jesus Christ to be fully God
- An estimated 50% of Christian men struggle with pornography
- Religiously conscious girls are only 14% more likely to remain virgins than nonreligiously conscious girls

I have been unable to find statistics that reveal the percentage of people attending church on a regular basis who frequently engage in gossip, slander, fits of rage, verbal abuse, indecent behavior, foul language, greed, laziness, gluttony, apathy, conceit, complacency, arrogance, etc. I think it is safe to assume that the numbers are higher than we would want to reveal on a national survey.

Shouldn't we look and behave much better than we do? Chuck Colson once said, "We are still living in a society were the main religious creed is Christianity, and our private morality is primarily a revolt against Christian morality."

Whenever I behave in a way that grieves the heart of God I must admit that I am behaving instead in a way that excites the seditious nature of Satan. Whether conscious or unconscious, my revolt against God is willful compliance with the enemy of God. In fact, whenever I choose to sin, I imitate the defiance that first began the battle between good and evil.

THE SATANISH WAYS OF SIN

As I have tried to imagine what the actions of Satan looked like at the time of his rebellion, I have been stunned by how similar to Satan I am behaving when I choose to disobey the voice of God. When Satan said, "I will be like God," he revealed some disturbing things about the nature of evil. His revulsion at the thought of being dependent on a higher power for care, protection, and direction provoked him to rage against his own inability to act independently within the kingdom. He was repulsed by the idea of having to serve someone other than himself, so he set himself up as his own authority. He hated the word *no*. He was thrilled when a band of his fellow angels affirmed his anger by following him out of heaven. And he was envious of the worship being given to the One who had created him.

When I am honest about my sin I am obliged to concede that I am doing what the angels who left their Creator did. I am following the wrong god.

It's like a story I heard many years ago of a woman who came home with an expensive fur coat. As she modeled it before her dumfounded husband, she said, "At first I thought it was too ostentatious for a woman like me. But then I heard a little voice telling me that I deserved to have it, so I walked right up to the counter and said, 'Ring it up!'"

Her husband questioned her impulsive decision, "Why didn't you just say, 'Get thee behind me, Satan'?"

"I did," she replied, "but then he said, 'It looks pretty good from back here too,'... so I bought it!" If I am going to be successful at hearing and obeying the voice of my *true* leader, I need to know exactly who my leader is, what He is like, and how to resist being fooled by cheap imitations.

God loves me. He loved me before I was born and He loves me now. It has been His intention from the beginning of time to share eternity with me. I have always been in His heart. It was because of His passionate desire to call me His daughter that He sent Jesus to die for my sin. His love compels Him to be merciful toward me and to shower me with forgiveness every single day. He has given gifts to me that have the potential to provide valuable services for the sake of His kingdom. He sees me as already perfect in His sight, even though I often fail to live up to His standards. He loves my love for Him. He is my Dad. He is crazy about me even when I can't stand myself. Nothing I do ever surprises Him or causes Him to rub His forehead wondering why He ever gave me a moment's notice. Instead, He keeps the gates of heaven polished and ready to swing open when I take my last breath here on earth.

This same selfless affection and purity of character cannot, however, be said of Satan. There is nothing about me that Satan finds appealing. He hates me! I am detestable to him! I am just a means to his real goal—to satisfy his revenge against the One whom he can never be like by destroying all that the Father loves—Jesus, His church, His kingdom, and me. Though Satan has the power to do many things, his power runs short of being able to say *no* to himself, to seek the good of others, to know joy, or to forgive sin. He is the father of lies, the inspiration of evil, and the organizer of destruction. His complete self-centeredness renders him useless in the love department. Because he hasn't the capacity to love anyone other than himself, he cannot love me. Nothing he touches escapes corruption. He hungers to fill his kingdom with the skeletons of the Master's children.

> But if serving the LORD seems undesirable to you, then choose for yourselves this day whom you will serve. (Joshua 24:15, NIV)

REBELLION—KEY TO A SINGLE-HEARTED LOVE FOR CHRIST

Rebellion is no small issue to our holy God. In fact, God equates acts of rebellion with witchcraft and idolatry. Rebellion against the commands, the principles, and the standards of our Master is mutiny against His position, His power, and His love. God has made His intentions perfectly clear. He has told us that we are never to rebel against Him. But has He told us that we are never to rebel against sin? No. In fact, He has told us that we are to flee from it, to run from it, to shut the door against it, to say no to it whenever the opportunity to sin is presented to us. Because the payment for our sin came at such a high price, continuing to succumb to sin behaviors trivializes the victory that He has won on our behalf.

Have you ever considered what would have happened to

Satan's plans if all the angels in heaven had said no to his bid for their allegiance? If Eve had turned her back on the serpent's sales pitch to pick fruit off the forbidden tree, how powerful would his presence be in the world today? What would happen right now if you and I made a purposeful choice to rebel against the enemy's fraudulent rule over our lives? A leader without followers is like a bark without a dog.

Now I would not be so arrogant as to presume that sin could ever be removed by an act of our human will. But God has provided a way for us to loosen the grip it has on our lives. That way began with the sacrifice of Jesus Christ, who put our sin to death on the cross. His death not only conquered sin; it also fitted us with a new, incorruptible nature residing within us through the Holy Spirit of God. It is this power that equips us to do battle with the corruptible nature of our flesh.

This was a most confusing issue for me when I first gave my heart to the Master. I didn't know whom to blame for my failure to live up to God's standards. I chastised myself for being too weak to resist the temptations that were continuously parading themselves before me. In the secret places of my mind I questioned the reality of my salvation, and wondered if God was really there at all.

But God was there. I had been looking at my battle with sin as something that I needed to do for God rather than something God desired to do for me. My on-going war with sin could only be won through the power of Christ living in me. The truth of the matter is: I *am* too weak on my own to resist sin, but I can choose to yield the battle to God so that He can win the battle through me. Each time I choose to cooperate with Him by obeying His directives I discover how wonderful the thrill of His victory is.

Obedience is the goal of our rebellion. Step one toward obedience begins with a hearty agreement that sin is contrary to God's will for our lives. Step two requires us to turn our backs against the author of sin—Satan. Whatever steps follow are the steps of obedience, walked out in faith, following the One who came as our example for holy living. This process works. If we stumble along the way, we need to go back to step one and begin again. Jesus is the champion of new beginnings.

We are in a war. A battle is being waged for our souls. I believe with every fiber in my being that rebellion is not only necessary for all Christian women today, it is imperative. A call is being sounded for our obedience. A choice needs to be made as to whose voice we will hear and pledge our allegiance to.

DOING BATTLE

Throughout this book I have consistently chosen to refer to God as the *Master* and to Satan as the *Impostor*. I have purposefully done this because it is the clearest way to distinguish between the One who has a right to our obedience and the one who merely pretends to have our best interests at heart.

The call to rebel against sin, I believe, is the key to a single-hearted love for Christ. Rebellion against sin declares that we are ready to change direction in our lives. Rebellion against sin strengthens our resolve to say no to the Impostor and to say yes to the Master. It frees us to love what God loves and hate what He hates. Each time we draw the line in the sand and make our declaration of war against sin clear, we affirm to our own spirit that we are choosing to take up arms with the Master in the battle for our souls.

I have had many opportunities to put rebellion against sin to the test. For years I struggled with the effects of a low self-image. My insecurities caused me to maintain a constant vigil over my feelings. One offhand comment from a friend, one misunderstanding, one failure to include me in a group activity and my emotions would spin out of control. While fussing over my wounds I would entertain slanderous thoughts against the person who had caused my pain. I hated the hours spent building mountains out of molehills but I didn't know how to stop.

Is low self-esteem sin? No. But my responses to it led me into a barrage of sinful behaviors. My insecurity caused me to see myself as the center of my attention. Keeping my focus on myself blinded me to the needs of others and worse, it cast a shadow over my view of God. I handed the Impostor all the time he needed to fill my thoughts with maudlin stories of how sad my life was. Anger ensued. Self-pity reigned. Then I read Jesus' words in Matthew 10:24: "A student doesn't get a better desk than her teacher. A laborer doesn't make more money than his boss. Be content—pleased, even—when you, my students, my harvest hands, get the same treatment I get. If they call me, the Master, 'Dungface,' what can the workers expect?" (*The Message*). The sinful behavior began when I made an idol of my needs and placed them ahead of my love for Jesus. If He could be hurt, insulted, abused, ignored and misunderstood, and die for the people who had injured Him, certainly I could endure a few minor bouts with a bruised ego.

I had some serious business to do with God. The call to

rebellion was critical to my freedom from the bondage I was in. First, I needed to see my sin from God's perspective. When I did, I found that my behavior was unworthy of His call on my life. The pain of what I had been doing broke my self-centered heart. It was the first time I actually experienced what oneness with God felt like, for I was seeing my sin from His perspective. Then, I needed to deal with the one that had helped me to dig the pit I had fallen into. Thus, I turned my back on the Impostor and refused to make excuses for my compliance with his self-centered ways.

With the first two steps completed, I found that my desire to do the right thing was burning a new passion for righteousness in my heart. I spent a considerable amount of time studying how Jesus behaved toward the people who followed Him. His pattern provided the perfect example for me to follow. How He spoke, how He touched, how He forgave, and how He expressed anger gave me a new way of dealing with others. I also discovered the joy of knowing who I am in Christ and how deep God's love for me is. Rebellion against sin worked. I seldom waste my valuable time worrying about my tender feelings. I am free to be hurt without craving revenge or retreat. And my friendships have more long-lasting potential now that my sensitivities have been given to the Master.

Rebellion against sin validates our repentance and confirms our desire for obedience. There can be no true love for Christ without obedience. Worship is impossible without obedience. Joy is nonexistent without obedience. Obedience announces our complete and utter helplessness to save ourselves, to forgive ourselves, and to live new and different lives. Obedience, therefore, necessitates acts of rebellion against anything that might lead us away from loving Christ with all our being.

One day I asked a friend who was in a heated battle with a particular sin if she was ready to obey God in that particular area of her life. Her answer was a clear and enthusiastic, "Yes."

Then I said, "Now, Cindy, the next time you are tempted to do this, what will you do?"

"I hope I will obey God," she said with a hint of helplessness in her voice.

"But, what if you don't obey God?"

"Well," she said, "I just hope God will help me not to do those things again."

"But what if you do, do them again?" I was feeling a bit flustered by this point.

"Well, I will just have to pray that I don't!"

We must have a plan! Can God be blamed for our inability to stand against the temptations that seek to entrap us on a daily basis? If we only say *yes* to God aren't we then saying *maybe* to His enemy? *Maybe* is a poor substitute for *no*. Jesus said that we are to *let our yes be yes and our no be NO*. When we say *yes* to the Master, we must seal our vows by turning to the Impostor and saying *no*.

One rainy afternoon I watched an example that illustrated for me what saying *no* looks like in an old movie called *The Principal*.

A LESSON ON SAYING *NO*

The principal stood before the assembly, knowing this was his last chance to make a difference in the school he had been called to lead. The audience included future drug addicts, rapists, hookers, and gangland criminals of America. They sneered at the principal in willful defiance.

As the principal faced the crowd of anarchists, he discovered something he didn't know he had—standards. For the first time in his life, he would take a stand on the right side of an issue. With courage foreign to him he approached the microphone. His stare cut through the hostility of the crowd. Then his nostrils flared and his voice growled two words that were to change the course of that school's history. "No more!"

"No more!"

No more would rebellious thugs run the school. *No more* would the education of students be left to gang members who owned the streets. *No more* would the teaching staff tolerate insubordinate behavior from their students. *No more* would the rules of his school be optional! The list of new regulations ran off his tongue with passionate resolve—*no drugs, no guns, no cigarettes, no fighting in the halls*. The speech continued, "No more, no more, no more." The line of demarcation had been drawn. The standard had been set. The time to take action was at hand. A new kind of rebellion was about to begin!

The purpose of this book is to build rebels—women who will step up to the microphone, clear their throats, stand before the Impostor, and say, *No more!*

No more will you dictate the affections of my heart!

No more will you take up residence in my home!

No more will you be the director of my focus!

No more will you choose my friends, my profession, or my activities!

No more will you attend church with me!

No more, no more, no more!

But the people who know their God will firmly resist him. (Daniel 11:32b)

THE WHY AND WHO OF REBELLION

Perhaps you have not yet seen a reason good enough for you to continue reading this book. Let me give you three more ideas.

First, we need to become rebels for the sake of our own souls. There is a great uneasiness in women today. The more we search for security and purpose, the more we feel drained and disquieted. We will examine the many reasons for this discontentment in greater detail as we move throughout the chapters of this book. Wherever there is confusion, chaos, frustration, dissatisfaction, or restlessness, the Impostor is at the center of the problem. The fruit of the Spirit, which is the evidence of a life transformed by the Master's touch, can never be brought to fruition when watered from the Impostor's well. He needs to be escorted out of our gardens if we are to bear good fruit.

Second, we need to become rebels for the sake of the church. With so much talk about revival and so little evidence to support it, many Christians are waiting for God to shake them awake and usher in a type of renewal that will make Christianity feel better than it feels now. We have allowed our faith to be primarily based on our feelings—either the *feel good* kind or the *feel bad* kind. Spiritual apathy, spiritual abuses, spiritual quackery, and spiritual snobbery has the church unraveling at the edges. The church is the great love of the Master's heart. Although revival is what many people are hoping for, perhaps rebellion against sin is the needed prescription for what ails us. When the world looks at the church they should not see their own reflection. Instead, the church should stand as a mirror of Christ in the lives of His people.

We can neither survive nor thrive without the body of Christ. Christians do not have the luxury of living like hermits. We need each other so we can help each other grow into wise, mature, respectable individuals who, when we come together, look like Jesus. The Master has fashioned us in such a way that on our own we can only reflect a portion of the body of Christ. But when we come together in love and unity, we become the full body of Christ. Eyes, ears, voice, hands, and feet, we complete the picture of Jesus when we lock arms in one common purpose—to spread His love everywhere! Growth of this kind may not always *feel* good, but there is one thing of which we can be certain...it will always *do* good!

Third, we need to become rebels for the sake of the Master Himself. In the great parable of the prodigal son, we see a portrait of the Master's heart. When the rebellious son grabbed his inheritance and left his father's home, he broke his father's heart. The lonely dad stood on a hill day after day waiting for his son to return. The pain of separation weighed heavily on him, knowing that the world was eager to devour the child whom he had raised with such great wisdom and kind affection. Finally, the day came when the father saw a shadow advancing from around the bend. His heart pounded in suspense. Then, in moments that must have felt like a lifetime, he could see the form of a young man. It was him! The delight of the father's heart could not be contained. He ran to meet him. Love showered tears over the prodigal until he was drenched in the sweetness of their reconciliation. A feast was prepared to welcome him home. The father's grief melted away in the joy of seeing his son who was lost and now was found.

The Word of God warns that we must be careful not to

grieve the heart of God. Yet, every time we wander away from Him and follow the whims of the Impostor, we become a source of pain to the One who loves us deeply; we cause Him grief. The woman who has just been widowed, the mother who has felt her child's life slip away from her, the girl who has said good-bye to her beloved daddy as he left their home for the last time; these all have experiential understanding of the pain that grief brings.

Each time we put Him on hold, we reject the love He desires to lavish upon us. This is the third, and I believe the most important reason that can be given for heeding God's call to rebellion. We must, for the sake of the Master, stand against anyone or anything that would inflict sorrow upon the greatest love we have and can ever know. The time to rebel is at hand!

This holy rebellion, however, cannot be launched until we, as women, take a purposeful look at our lives. Throughout this book we will sort through the many facets of our lives and draw a line of distinction that will identify where and how the Impostor has affected the way we think, feel, and behave. We will discover together that Christianity is *Christ-in-you-ity*. It is found in our *being* before it appears in the *doing*. We will untwist the message of the Impostor and fine-tune the message of the Master. We will seek to rekindle the flame of holy passion and send it soaring through the gates of heaven as a fragrant aroma to the God who is worthy of our loyal, unfettered, wholehearted, fully devoted service and affection.

Now, before you enlist in the Master's army thinking that you are able on your own to do battle with the Impostor, let me encourage you for a moment to pause and consider what the uniform you are about to put on looks like. It consists of a pair of army boots waiting to be filled with the Master's feet so that the message of His love can be marched throughout your sphere of influence. It is a helmet waiting to cover you with the Master's authority. It is a shield of faith waiting for the Master's strength to hold it. It is a belt waiting to be fastened by the Master's truth. It is a breastplate waiting to be polished with the Master's character. It is a sword waiting to be sharpened by the Master's words. And it is a battle that is supported by prayer for the Master's power and seal of approval. You and I can do nothing on our own. The Master, who has called us, will be the One to equip us and make us ready for battle. The way, the means, and the victory all belong to Him.

The Master wants you! Prepare yourself to heed the call of rebellion so that you might experience the joy of having a single-hearted love for Christ!

PART ONE

*Single-Hearted Love
for Christ*

The Chosen Heart

But you are a chosen people,
a royal priesthood, a holy nation.
A people belonging to God,
that you may declare the praises of him
who called you out of darkness
into his wonderful light.

1 PETER 2:9, NIV

*I*t was her night for miracles—the night when a common chore girl became a princess. With the touch of the fairy godmother's wand, her tattered dress was transformed into a glimmering pink gown, a pumpkin was converted into a grand coach, and six little mice were changed into dashing white horses. Nearing the castle, the sound of a thousand strings filled the air with music. The glass slippers that fit so perfectly on her feet were ready to dance.

Cinderella's heart fluttered with excitement as she entered the castle. There, overlooking the ballroom from the balcony, she stood mesmerized by the splendor of the scene that unfolded below. Couples danced effortlessly around the room in costumes adorned with jewels that flickered like tiny lights shimmering against the night. Within moments the waltz twirled slowly to a halt while the music faded to a whisper. A hush fell across the room. Cinderella began to blush as the guests turned their attention toward her. Emerging from within the crowd, the prince appeared. With the confidence of a king and the wonder of a boy, he held out his hand and escorted her to the center of the ballroom floor. One cue to the conductor and the music resumed. Cinderella was dancing in the arms of the prince. The love sparkling in their eyes told the bewildered guests that the contest was over—the prince had found his princess.

It was the perfect love story—undeserving girl meets handsome prince and in an instant her life was changed from a hopeless here and now to a happy ever after. Out of all the women at the ball, the prince, who deemed her worthy to be his princess bride, had chosen her.

As Christian women, you and I have experienced, at least to some degree, the joy of dancing in Cinderella's slippers. Long before we knew Him, God turned His eyes toward us and selected us to be His own beloved daughters. He reached out, took our helpless faces in His warm hands, and said, "I love you. You're the one I've chosen. You're my heart's desire." The Creator of the entire universe pulled us out of the crowd, escorted us to the dance floor, and proved to the world that we are a treasured possession, a person of value, and a woman of worth.

> How blessed is God! And what a blessing he is! He's the Father of our Master, Jesus Christ, and takes us to the high places of blessing in him. Long before he laid down earth's foundations, he had us in mind, had settled on us as the focus of his love, to be made whole and holy by his love. Long, long ago he decided to adopt us into his family through Jesus Christ. [What pleasure he took in planning this!] He wanted us to enter into the celebration of his lavish gift-giving by the hand of his beloved Son. (Ephesians 1:3–8, *The Message*)

Long before we came to the ball, we were not only in His mind, we were the objects of His love and the passion of His longing. He wrote the script for our love story before we had even an inkling of what true love looked like. It was His decision to adopt us into His family, to make us heirs to His kingdom, and to shower us with all the blessings that are appropriate for the children of nobility. Everything that belongs to Jesus was handed to us—just for the asking. It was His gift. He chose us so that we could choose Him.

As a little girl I was charmed by the tale of Cinderella. Her story gave me hope that some day my prince would come and with the touch of his hand brush away all the hurt, fear, and inadequacy that plagued my childlike heart. My prince came, but the purpose for his appearance surprised me. I longed for a rescuer; instead I found a redeemer.

I was fourteen years old when a friend from school asked me if I knew Jesus Christ as my personal Savior. Her question stunned me. I had attended church often while growing up and it never occurred to me that going to church might be different than actually knowing Jesus. Laura was a tenacious evangelist. She shared the gospel with me. For the first time I understood why Jesus had to die for my sin and how His death was my provision for eternal life. That night I knelt beside my bed and asked Jesus to come into my heart, forgive me for all of my sins, make me His child, and make my heart His home. I accepted His invitation to spend eternity with Him. My fear of eternal judgement was taken away, and I knew for the first time what joy felt like.

In one night, through one prayer, my life was changed forever. My prince had come, not dressed in the finest of satins, but clothed in wood, splattered with His own blood so that I could wear His righteous clothing. I was no longer the child of that family down the street whose father was an alcoholic and where abuse and depression lived, but I was the child of God. I was the daughter of the King of all kings. His adoption of me authenticated His love for me. I felt warm and secure in the love of my heavenly Father. The Bible made sense to me. I loved going to church. I cared about my family's eternal destiny. I enjoyed the company of my new Christian friends. The gospel was no longer an old story told in a dust-covered book on a shelf—it was personal. I had a new life and a new identity. I inherited the name of the One who saved me—*Christ*-ian.

> That's plain enough, isn't it? You're no longer wandering exiles. This kingdom of faith is now your home country. You're no longer strangers or outsiders. You belong here, with as much right to the name Christian as anyone. (Ephesians 2:19, *The Message*)

That is what God has done for you when you become His daughter. When He chose you to be His child, He authenticated His love for you by sending Jesus to die for you. You are His. He knows you through and through. He will never tear up your adoption papers. You will always be His. No matter how often you fail to live up to His standards, He will never give up on you because He sees you through His Son. The perfect, sinless record of Jesus Christ is your record. Ponder this brief list of what this means for you and me as the chosen daughters of God.

- You are a chosen daughter and dearly loved by God. (Ephesians 1:4)
- You are a joint heir with Christ, sharing His righteousness with Him. (Romans 8:17)
- You have been made alive with Christ who has forgiven all your sins. Your debt has been cancelled. (Colossians 2:13–14)
- You are forever free from condemnation. (Romans 8:1)
- You may approach the throne of grace with confidence to receive mercy and find grace to help in time of need. (Hebrews 4:16)
- You are a member of God's own people, a royal priesthood, a people for God's own possession. (1 Peter 2:9–10)
- You have received the Spirit of God into your life so you can understand what God has freely given you. (1 Corinthians 2:12)
- You have been given His exceedingly great and precious promises so you may participate in His holy nature and escape the corruption in the world. (2 Peter 1:4)
- You are secure in Christ. Nothing will be able to separate you from the love of God that is in Christ Jesus your Lord. (Romans 8:39)
- You are a saint. (Ephesians 1:1)[1]

It would be wonderful if I could say to you with a straight face that ever since the day I gave my heart to Jesus I have always *felt* like I was His child. I wish I could say I always *feel* worthy to be called His precious daughter, His treasured possession, or His holy one. I don't, because being chosen goes far beyond the realm of what I *feel* or don't *feel* at any given moment. It is the unconditional and unchangeable love of Christ, my Savior, which has made the gospel God's real-life love story for me.

MORE THAN A FEELING

Let's go back for a moment and take another look at the story of Cinderella and her prince. Their love at first sight experience turned an animated cartoon into a classic movie hit. But it might not be the best illustration to use when searching for the meaning of true love. After all, it was all too quick and impetuous. One glance at a pretty face and the prince was ready to commit his life and his castle to a nameless girl who walked in late for the ball. And as for Cinderella—what kind of a romantic bubble-head runs off with a guy who looks great in a suit so she can escape a troubled home environment? With a foundation as shaky as theirs, it wouldn't be too surprising if the sequel to their story went something like this:

Cinderella II: Far beyond the Honeymoon

In this episode we find poor Cindy standing on the balcony of the castle, looking out over the gardens with a tear hanging off her quivering chin. Shooing the crows away from her English muffins, she sings into the breeze that old Barbra Striesand/Neil Diamond tune, *"You don't bring me flowers, You don't sing me love songs…"*

Somewhere in the woods, Mr. Prince sits on a log crooning right back at her,

"You never run to me anymore, when I walk through the door at the end of the day."

Maybe Cinderella and her prince were discovering what

we all find out sooner or later—feelings are fickle. The needle on our emotional compass has the capacity to change direction in just a snap of a finger. When our prince comes home hiding a bouquet of roses behind his back we look at him and think he's the most adorable creature ever made. But after the kiss, when he asks what's for dinner, that adorable creature isn't quite as adorable as he was just seconds before. No wonder the old saying says that there is a fine line between love and hate. Feelings are unreliable sources to count on when we want the reality of our love to be confirmed.

Most of us have no problem feeling confident about God's eternal love for us when life is going just the way we want it to go. But, when the clouds of crisis come storming toward us and it seems that God has taken a vacation, our confidence can easily be shattered in the blast—if, that is, we are placing our confidence in how we feel.

When I first began writing this book, I felt an overwhelming sense of certainty that I was doing exactly what God had called me to do. All of my friends agreed that not only was the subject inspired but that I was the one God had chosen to proclaim it. Shortly after I sent the first draft off to a variety of publishers, a well-respected publishing house picked up the manuscript and held it under consideration for seven months. During that time it appeared a contract was eminent. While it looked as if my book was going to be published, I experienced the most extraordinary feelings of passion, peace, contentment, and joy. Then, on a cold day in November, a call from the publishers ended my brief appointment with success. My book was rejected. I felt rejected. I questioned whether I had really heard from God or not. The thought of having spent an entire year wasting my time pounding meaningless words into my computer left me feeling utterly humiliated.

It took me three days to get the courage to face God with my heart's deepest questions. *Oh, God, what have I done? Did I hear you right? I am sorry to be such a dunderhead right now but I need you to be very clear with me. What do you want me to do? I will do whatever you ask, but please, O God, make Your way known to me.*

The next day during my quiet time, God spoke. I was reminded that I was indeed chosen by God and that this truth is the foundation of my salvation and the basis of everything I believe. Then, as I went to prayer, the first three chapters of my book unfolded before me revealing what needed to be done to strengthen their message. Finally, I picked up my Bible and opened to the place where I had left off the day before—2 Corinthians 8:11–12 and read: "Now finish the work, so that your eager willingness to do it may be matched by your completion of it, according to your means. For if the willingness is there, the gift is acceptable according to what one has, not according to what he does not have." I was deeply moved.

In June of the following year, I received a phone call from Multnomah Publishers asking me to come to Sisters to discuss *Called to Rebellion*. Had I listened to my feelings during my time of crisis, I would have missed the blessing of hearing God's voice and receiving His tender compassion and encouragement. I would have stopped the work that I felt so passionately called to do. And I would have allowed the Impostor to tell me that I was a fool to believe that God could ever use me to write anything worth reading. I went back to my office with a renewed zeal to complete the task at hand and a deep sense that God had used these experiences to sharpen me so that I could serve Him better.

It is far too easy to use our feelings as a thermometer to gauge God's love for us. Discouragement, disappointment, anger, and even the death of a vision may cast grim shadows on our emotions and hide God's promise to never leave us or toss us aside. But God's promises are never ruled by our feelings.

We may hope the joy of being chosen will last forever, but the truth is—it doesn't. So, during those times when our feelings change and the pitter doesn't patter anymore, we need to go back to the dance floor and recapture what really happened the night we were swept away by the King of our hearts. What was it that He did? Who did He say we were?

BEYOND THE FAIRYTALE

Everything changed for Cinderella when the clock struck twelve on the night of the ball. Horses went back to being mice again, the coach turned into a pumpkin, and Cinderella's glittering gown faded away. Donned in her tattered dress, she picked up her mop and dust cloth and tried as best she could to put the night of her dreams behind her. But the love the prince had for his fair maiden would not be thwarted. Though her stepmother and the two ugly stepsisters tried to keep her hidden—he found her. Though she felt unworthy of his love—his love won her. There was nothing she could do to discourage the prince from loving her with all his heart. The perfection of his affection drew her near and persuaded her that they were meant to be together.

What a life Cinderella had been chosen for! The ragamuffin

stepchild became a stately member of the royal family with a royal family identity and royal family responsibilities. But there must have been times when flashbacks of her life before the castle caused her to wonder if she would ever really become the princess the fairytale claimed her to be.

After the honeymoon period of my new life in Christ was over, the reality of learning how to live like a Christian left me feeling like the new kid in school.

One of my struggles was believing God's promises to me, and this, no doubt, was linked to patterns of thinking I'd developed living with an alchoholic father. When God said He would love me with an everlasting love, I automatically put conditions and limits to His words. When He said that nothing could ever separate me from His love, I took my name out of the text and inserted the names of other more deserving Christians instead. When He said that He would meet all my needs, answer all my prayers, and guard all my steps I held on to my trusty "no, not today" to cushion the blow of whatever disappointments I feared would come. The Impostor had easy access to my reservoir of fear and my inability to surrender the control of my life to the Master.

It took years of allowing God to show me, one prayer at a time, how faithful and trustworthy He is. I have often recorded the wonderful accounts of answered prayer and read them over whenever I felt that He would not continue to love me through my periods of wavering faith. Now I have more undeniable experiences of God's reliable promises than I have of my father's ill-fated intentions.

I also had a chronic love for attention. My ability to make people laugh and charm crowds served me well in our home and with my friends, and this ability almost always secured the leading parts in school plays. Though humor was God's gift to me to help me survive the tough times in life, it also became a source of egotistical pride and provided me with a false sense of security. As long as I could win people over, I could regulate the way they treated me or at least pretend that I could.

I vacillated between my craving to be up front and my new hyperspiritual fear of being seen as a show off. I mistrusted my motives and scrutinized my behavior with dogged perfectionism. The Impostor couldn't have been more pleased with my confusion; I was just how he wanted me to be—unproductive in the Master's kingdom.

Today I find enormous freedom in serving Christ through the gifts He has given me. I realize that none of my talents have come to me through my own inspired genius. All that I am has been chosen beforehand by the Master. God has authorized my gifts to be used to delight, inspire, encourage, and motivate others. I no longer worry about my motives. Though I am still constrained to examine the condition of my heart regarding holiness, I experience great joy in doing what I have been created to do.

I had huge concerns also that my life would forever be tied to my past, and I battled feelings of anger toward my parents for the way I had been raised. Psychologists, psychiatrists, and social workers all agreed that a child born in an abusive home was bound to become an abuser also. Their well-meaning predictions painted a very dark future for me. Though I tried to keep my bouts with depression hidden, my thoughts were often haunted by the memories of terror in the night and the feeling of hopelessness that followed me through the day.

Though I was determined to never repeat the mistakes of my family, I felt powerless to stop the patterns that had already begun to show themselves in my temperament. I had a difficult time knowing how to turn those patterns around. Instead of trusting God with my life, I was often fearful that God would grow weary of my backward turns and give up on me altogether. As long as the Impostor was able to keep me focused on my inadequacies and failures, I remained blinded to the Master's mercy and persistent grace.

Then I came upon one of the most astounding word in Scripture—*but*.

> *But* you are A CHOSEN RACE, A royal PRIESTHOOD, A HOLY NATION, A PEOPLE FOR *God's* own POSSESSION, that you may proclaim the excellencies of Him who has called you out of darkness into His marvelous light; for you once were NOT A PEOPLE, *but* now you are THE PEOPLE OF GOD; you had NOT RECEIVED MERCY, *but* now you have RECEIVED MERCY. (1 Peter 2:9–10, NASB, emphasis mine)

This three-letter word told me that no matter what my life had been; it was now changed. Because I have been chosen to be a child of God, I am no longer tied to my past. God is faithfully, every day, doing a new thing in me. Each day of being His child provides me with more opportunities to allow Him to pour more of His character into my personality. Once I had no purpose for living, *but* today I have the esteemed privilege of declaring His truth to an unbelieving world. Once I had no real identity, *but* today I am a child of God's eternal kingdom. Once I had no hope of mercy, *but* today I am drenched in it. Through the wisdom of His word, His thoughts continue to become my thoughts, teaching me daily how to live.

Being chosen is not just a feeling; it is a fact. No matter how warm and fuzzy I might or might not *feel* about the presence of God in my life and no matter how secure I might *feel* regarding my position in Him—He has declared by His own words who I am. My new life and my new identity are not subject to the infidelity of my feelings. All that I am has been firmly established from the very beginning of time. I am His. It's more than a fairytale; it's the core of my existence.

A BETTER LOVE STORY

When Cinderella fled the scene that night at the ball, the only clue the prince had to help him find her again was the fragile glass slipper that fell from her foot while she ran. So determined was he to find the love of his life that he went door to door searching for the woman whose shoe size would be a perfect fit. Fat feet, skinny feet, stinky feet, and feet needing some serious pedicures, told the prince that his search would not be easy.

Then, when he thought that he couldn't stand one more disappointment, he knocked on the last door in the village. Greeting him at the threshold was the most beautiful chore girl he had ever seen. Cinderella's cheeks grew hot with embarrassment. The ruse was up. Her true identity was exposed and there was nowhere to run. Yet, without a moment's hesitation the prince presented the slipper to his runaway princess. Her foot slipped easily into the crystal shoe. The prince swept her up in his arms and carried her off to his castle to begin the new life for which she had been chosen.

The joy of our love story is that is goes on forever. The matchless love of God is a perfect fit for the heart that has been redeemed by the Savior. What God has chosen will never be rejected. It is easy to lose sight of God's undying, eternal love for us if we allow the Impostor to hold our imperfections before us and taunt us with arguments like: "Look how bad you've been…See how you failed…? You'll never amount to anything…Why can't you be more like…? You don't deserve to be loved…"

Charles Spurgeon described this inward wrenching of the soul in words that seem to have been salted with the tears of one who experienced the battle firsthand.

> Do you not feel in your own soul that perfection is not in you? Does not every day teach you that? Every tear trickling from your eye, weeps "imperfection"; every sigh bursting from your heart, cries "imperfection"; every harsh word proceeding from your lip, mutters "imperfection." You have had a view of your own heart too frequently to dream for a moment of any perfection in yourself. But amid this sad consciousness of imperfection, here is comfort for you—you are "perfect in Christ." In God's sight, you are "complete in Him"; even now you are "accepted in the beloved.
>
> With my Savior's garments on,
> Holy as the Holy One.
> …Then we shall know, and taste, and feel the happiness of the vast but short sentence, "Complete in Christ."[2]

When darkness seeks to overwhelm my soul with pictures of my imperfections and evidences of my failures and when it seems my hope has drizzled down to a single rain-drop, I have nothing left to cling to but the most basic truths of the Master. Has He ever failed me? Has He ever disregarded my most desperate needs? Has He ever closed the door to my visits or covered His ears to my cries for help? No. He can love me with everlasting love because He has clothed me with *His* perfection. I *am* perfect now in Christ. I am already free from the penalty of sin. Nothing that pertains to sin will fol-low me into heaven. How can I fully grasp the wonder of this kind of love?

> What marvelous love the Father has extended to us! Just look at it—we're called children of God! That's who we really are. But that's also why the world doesn't recognize us or take us seriously, because it has no idea who he is or what he's up to. But friends, that's exactly who we are: children of God. And that's only the beginning. Who knows how we'll end up! What we know is that when Christ is openly revealed, we'll see him—and in seeing him, become like him. All of us who look forward to his Coming stay ready, with the glistening purity of Jesus' life as a model for our own. (1 John 3:1–3, *The Message*)

Our story is better than Cinderella's. You and I are imper-fect women chosen by a perfect God who has wrapped us in His perfection and put us on His path to eternal life where happy ever after has no ending. But beware—there is one who lurks around the corner impersonating the Master. He will do all he can to distract you from the truth and to keep you from knowing the fullness of the life the Faithful Master has called you to live.

What is this fullness of life that Jesus promised to bring us? I doubt that Jesus was the least bit concerned with how many worldly treasures He could add to our temporal bank accounts. As I have tried to assess my life in terms of this promise, what I have come to realize is that His gifts to me are found in unseen yet vividly recognized testimonies of His presence in me. In times of indecision or crisis, He gives me wisdom, not because He *has* wisdom but because He *is* wisdom. He fills my life with joy, not because He has lots of joy to give, but because He is the fountain from which joy springs. He strengthens me with power, not because He has enough power to spare, but because He Himself *is* the power source. And He covers me with peace, not because He has some extra peace on hand, but because He *is* peace. This is the fullness of life that Jesus promised to give—it is His life in us given without reservation or reluctance.

The last thing the Impostor wants is for us to be secure in the love of the Master. If we are sure to whom we belong and where our hope is found we will grow, blossom, and mature in our walk with Christ. Our lives will reflect Him in everything we do. Other people will know who our God is. And the Imposter's task of derailing us on the road to heaven will be thwarted.

Because ours is a superior love story, it merits a more excellent life from we who have been called to be the children of God. We have been chosen by the Master. Now the question we must address is: *Are we ready to choose Him? Are we ready to commit our way to Him? Are we ready to seek Him with all our heart, mind and spirit? Are we ready to pay close attention to how we are living?* He has already given us the clothing and the tools we need to rebel against His enemy. We are already armed with the power we need to win the war for the affection of our hearts. We need now to resolve to move forward as we allow the truths that He has given us to permeate every area of our being.

> *We must pay more careful attention, therefore,*
> *to what we have heard, so that we do not drift away.*

HEBREWS 2:1

One Heart, One Master

As long as Jesus is one of many options,
He is no option.

MAX LUCADO, *THE APPLAUSE OF HEAVEN*

omen who have had babies seem to have a common love for sharing their childbirth horror stories. I've had two babies with no horror stories to tell. Both of my children came into the world via Caesarian section. The response I often receive when my turn comes to tell my tales of doing hard time in the delivery room goes something like this: "Oh, you lucky thing, you got to take the easy way out."

For the three years following the birth of our daughter, Annette, I felt as if everything I had prepared for, including that last push and the sound of my child crying for the first time, had been stolen from me. Instead, I was wheeled into a sterile room where a team of medical experts gathered around my tummy, cut me open, and lifted my child out of my body. Not one of them acknowledged my presence. No one said, "How are you doing, Mrs. Snavely? What are you hoping for, a boy or a girl?" Moreover, after they delivered my precious cargo, they forgot to tell me whether I was the mother of a girl person or a boy person or if all they found in there was a bunch of bananas.

Three years later I became pregnant with our son, Dean. No matter how much I loved being pregnant, every time I looked toward my baby's due date, a feeling of regret would swallow up my joy. Then as I neared the end of my eighth month, Dr. Cohen—my new obstetrician—looked at me and said, "Sandy, is there anything bothering you about the delivery of your child?"

I started to cry and told him how unfulfilling my last delivery had been. After I finished getting dressed I met Dr. Cohen in his office for a heart-to-heart chat about childbirth. He took a large book down from a shelf and proceeded to show me what a delivery by Caesarian section looks like. It was fascinating. Approximately five, clear plastic pictures representing the various stages of a typical C-section covered a full colored picture of a mother's womb. Dr. Cohen carefully explained the surgical procedure as he lifted each transparency. By the time the last transparent picture was lifted, I had a clear understanding of how my child would be born. Dr Cohen promised me that he would not allow anyone to leave me out of the birth process. He kept his promise.

As I think back to my doctor's graphic account of childbirth, one illustration continues to amaze me. After the pictures of the woman's abdomen and the layers of tissue covering the unborn child were lifted away, the last transparency revealed the most remarkable miracle of life. The mother's womb was perfectly configured to accommodate the life of the baby nestled inside of her. There the baby lay peacefully sucking its thumb while the mother provided everything it needed—food, water, space, protection, and love. The picture was so ideal that one could almost wonder why the baby would ever want to live anywhere else.

I know that when I gave my heart to Jesus I started out in the right place. A holy, just, and loving heavenly Father chose me to be His wonderful child. From the moment Jesus received me into His kingdom, I have been a perfect fit for His perfect heart. Each day He gives me everything I need to live. Love, joy, peace, patience, kindness, goodness, gentleness, longsuffering, and the ability to control myself is all mine without restrictions as long as I am willing to be conformed to the configuration of His heart. It's when I start searching for something other than what the Master has offered me that I end up looking for a space of my own where I can spread my wings and fly. The problem is that without the configuration of God's heart, I have no guidelines to help me know where and how I fit into this life He has called me to. A heart that is contrary to the contour of the Master's heart is a heart that is made to order for the Impostor.

I have often been plagued with the feeling that I am unfit for the Master's heart. The result of my insecurity unwittingly turns my focus in the wrong direction. I become the center of my own existence. I begin to overextend myself by setting unrealistic goals, hoping to achieve relevant results. I search for ways to satisfy my need for significance and fulfillment. No matter how benevolent my activities may appear to others, they are nonetheless driven by my instinctive need to be well-thought-of for my own name's sake. I become so overcome with my own inadequacies that I forget where my sufficiency is found.

This became obvious to me one day while conversing with my sister Rosanne on the phone. When we were young Christian women, Rosanne and I would often compete with each other in the exhausting game of "Top This If You Can." During one such conversation, after Rosanne had finished rattling off her list of the wonderful things she was doing in her church, I matched my list with hers and topped it off with the wonderful things I was also doing in my neighborhood. Then, with the ball in her court, she hit back with the wonderful things she was doing with her children. I threw in my children and added the wonderful things I was doing with the children I also took care of in my home. Once we were finally exhausted with all the wonderful things we had each been doing we said good-bye. As I walked away from the phone I felt like I needed a nap. Why did talking to my sister always leave me feeling tired and frustrated?

My sister and I both loved God. We were each grateful for the new lives we had found through Jesus Christ. But beyond our gratitude we each were trying through our own efforts to fit the Master's heart into our hearts. God, however, never conforms Himself to a heart that is ruled by self. We were easy prey for the Impostor's crusade to derail the Master's children by keeping them preoccupied with themselves.

The Impostor's plan is clever. He knows there are certain unchangeable truths upon which our faith is founded and all of these truths center upon who the Master is and what He has done for us. He chose us to be His children. He never asked us to do anything to merit His unconditional love and affection. He gave us the gift of eternal life and paid the bill Himself. He has a mortgage free home in heaven waiting for us. And He lavishes His blessings on us every single day whether we ask Him to or not.

So it happens that the Imposter is found prowling around our lives waiting to steal these priceless gifts from us and waits for the opportunity to tarnish our joy. A little perversion of the truth here and a smidgen of twisting there and soon we find ourselves misunderstanding the things that should be easy for us to understand.

We might think—
Maybe I'm not really saved.
If I do good things, God will love me more.
God must really be angry with me for the things I am doing.
I've asked God to forgive me too many times.
If I only work a little harder, I will be good enough to be called
    a Christian.
God needs me to do His work for Him.
I'm not good enough.
I'm not smart enough.
The Christian life is just too hard to live up to.
Maybe God doesn't really exist at all.

The sound of these words is music to the Impostor's ears. He praises our efforts to earn God's favor, and he draws our focus away from the truth and onto ourselves. Just as the Impostor chose to live independently of God, he tempts us to do the same. Hovering around us as we seek to follow the way charted for us by the Master, the Impostor tirelessly plans our demise. He runs ahead of us rewriting the road signs and twisting the arrows away from the Master's heart. With his magic marker in hand, he writes over the signs provided for us in God's Word and then eagerly waits to watch us follow and fall. We've all seen his handiwork, haven't we? His signs all begin with self. One reads *Self-Satisfaction, This Way,* another, *Self-Empowerment, That Way.* More signs ahead read:

Self-Fulfillment,
Self-Awareness,
Self-Esteem.

And whatever else our *self* might desire.

The Impostor couldn't care less which of these we nibble on. As long as he can keep us on the futile search for our illusive self, a self which is impossible to find without Christ, he knows we will be diverted from following the Master's plan.

The Imposter has even provided examples of this phantom woman with the assistance of the media. Her pictures are everywhere. They're in our magazines, newspapers, televisions, and work places. They are in our churches and they are even in our homes.

These pictures portray her as consistently looking good on the outside and feeling good on the inside. Her kids love her, her husband adores her, her church admires her, her friends all want to be her, and the world, as we know it, couldn't survive without her. This woman is self-confident, self-accomplished, and self-directed. She is tailored, talented, and tempered. She knows how to wear the right suit, she has the right hair, and carries the right briefcase. She lives in the right condo, drives the right car, has the right kids in the right day care. She accessorizes with the right jewelry, her nails are perfect, and she has the right man on her arm. She is socially correct, politically correct, environmentally correct, and is often perceived as biblically correct. She is known for her courage and strength, her financial independence, power, and political prowess. She is a martyr. She knows when to be assertive and when to be coy. She can manage both people and circumstances and she can manipulate them all to her advantage whenever the need arises.

As I speak with other women, I find they are like me— tired of trying on their own to find contentment that can only be found in a heart that is fully surrendered to Christ. We are in a battle. This battle is not a conflict that centers on whether or not we, as women, will get our due respect and recognition. It is a spiritual battle between the Impostor and the Master.

Come join me for a moment in my imaginary theater and let's see what this battle for our hearts looks like.

The Battle for the Heart
A Play in three acts

Act I: Designed for Love

As Act I begins, we see the hands of the Master as He fashions a child. With tender devotion He weaves together one who will become a woman after His own heart. Upon the completion of His work, the Master sets her free to explore the world, which He has also made. Knowing His enemy will seek to entrap her, He sends His angels to guard her while she grows. Then He watches and waits for the appointed day when she will recognize the scarred hands of His Son who loved her enough to die for her. As the Holy Spirit calls her to come away from the world's ways and to give her heart fully to Him, the Master opens His arms to receive His beloved daughter. With new understanding she leaves behind the life she had designed for herself, places her tiny feet into His large footprints, and determines to follow her Master forever. Warm colors cast a peaceful glow across the stage. But before the audience begins to clap a dark shadow covers over the woman. She shivers slightly while the stage lights dim and the curtains are drawn on Act I.

Act II: Dancing with the Impostor

The curtain rises as a single spotlight reveals the Impostor who is crouched in the corner of the stage, rubbing his hands together and salivating with lust for the Master's creation while she sits unaware of his presence in the center of the stage. He clenches his fists in disgust as he watches her feasting on the delights of the Master's Word. Then with a snap of his fingers his clothing takes on the appearance of the Master's. With the approach that worked so well in the Garden, he slithers toward her and speaks in a soft voice, "What a lovely day it is." He grins as she innocently accepts his words as coming from the One who chose her and called her by name. The Impostor continues to toy with her, engaging her in a harmless assortment of random topics, until with subtle precision the Impostor asks, "Is this really enough for you?" Seeing that she is vulnerable to his voice he continues. "Are you sure that you are really mine? You seem to be dissatisfied and empty. I have many things for you to enjoy, but how can I lead you to them while you just sit here reading words that were written so long ago? It's time for you to discover who you really are."

A sound like shattering glass echoes through the theater. The peace that had radiated in the woman's face is gone. She begins to experience emotions she thought had been left behind when she gave her heart to the Master. Portraits of her own inadequacy flash before her. The same feelings of loneliness and insecurity that haunted her before the Master adopted her have returned to torment her. Acting on instinct, she follows the Impostor's lead, seeking to fill the void that is quickly taking over her heart. As she runs, confused and disoriented, a mournful voice calls out from the darkness that has now encircled the stage, "Come back. I'm waiting for you. Come back."

Act III: The Return of the Heart

Next we see a crowd of people rushing madly about the stage. Having been fooled into thinking she is following the Master, the woman tries her best to keep up with the pace being set by the purposeless throng. Motivated by the lies of the Impostor, she finds herself ensnared in the burdens fostered by the world's system. With invitations to serve herself, to seize every opportunity for success, and to gain whatever glory, power, and wealth that can be had, she has neither the time nor the inclination for prayerful introspection. Mixed in with the temporal pleasures she is striving to enjoy, she begins to sense within her heart a growing disillusionment with the course she has chosen.

Tiring quickly with his latest conquest, the Impostor moves to the left of the stage while taking one quick glance over his shoulder to make sure that the woman is still off course. Then he turns to the audience and grins. His eyes so pierce the crowd that many begin to squirm in their seats fearing that he might step off the stage and come after them. But the Impostor turns back to the people mulling about the stage and poses a familiar question to another unsuspecting child of the Master, "Is this really enough for you?"

At this point, a new twist to the plot begins to unfold as the spotlight shines on the woman of the Master. Crumbling under the weight of her worldly objectives and exhausted by her efforts to find true meaning for her life, the chosen one scans the stage in search of her Master. A look of terror comes across her face when she catches a glimpse of the Impostor, as he is about to add another casualty to the Master's list of new believers. She gasps in disbelief while she watches him changing into the Master's clothing. "It's you," she screams.

"You're the Impostor!" His charade exposed, the enemy coils toward her, mocking her words as she speaks them. "You're a liar. You're not my Master. You've been deceiving me with promises you can't fulfill. You have been stealing the Master's blessings from me. I don't belong to you anymore! I belong to Another. I will never be yours!"

Still trembling from the shock of her discovery, she turns away from the Impostor. With a cry of desperation the chosen one calls out for her Master as her knees begin to buckle. But before she hits the ground, He gently bends down to catch her. Safe in the arms of her Creator she buries her head in His nail pierced hands and weeps cleansing tears of repentance. Then the Master holds her close to His heart and speaks to her. "I love you unconditionally. I forgive you. You are mine. Stop striving and know that I am your God. Give Me your burdens and I will show you My sufficiency. Walk with Me and I will lead you home."

Once again walking with the One who loves her most, they leave the stage together. Before the curtains close on the third act a sinister growl erupts from deep within the Impostor. He summons his troops to begin a new crusade to steal her heart away from her Master.

THE STRATEGY OF THE IMPOSTOR

The third act is finished but the story goes on until the day when the Master escorts His chosen woman to her eternal home where the battle for her soul will be over, and she will be safe in His heavenly kingdom.

Prone to wander
Lord, I feel it

Prone to leave
This God I love.
Here's my heart
Oh take and seal it
Seal it for
Thy courts above.

"COME THOU FOUNT OF EVERY BLESSING"
ROBERT ROBINSON, 1758

Why are we so easily fooled by the lies of the Impostor as he entices us with empty promises and slings half-truths our way? When he says we don't have enough, we listen. When he says we need more, we ask, "How much?" Every time we respond to his words—each conversation we allow him to have with us—drives us farther from the sacrificial love of the Master to the egocentric love of self. Naïve to the Impostor's strategies, we strive to fill our own needs, seek to satisfy our own wants, and struggle to fulfill our own desires. This we do while often at the same time believing that we are serving and following the voice of the Master.

The Impostor may be cunning and conniving, but he is far from being stupid. He fully understands our position in Christ. He knows that when we receive Christ into our lives, we immediately become the legal heirs to the kingdom of God, and nothing will ever be able to separate us from that esteemed position (Romans 8:35–39). This fact leaves him but one option—to do whatever he can to cripple our walk with Christ. Hobbling around on our own, trying in our own strength to live a Christlike life is a good way to keep us from living fruitful lives. He knows that the Master's children can do nothing of real worth without the Master's power.

Therefore, the Impostor claims victory over us whenever he thinks he has robbed us of our godly significance as women, wives, mothers, homemakers, marketplace women, ministry workers, and friends.

Now, in case you might think that we are really special to merit so much attention from this unscrupulous enemy of God, think again. There is nothing about us that the Impostor loves or cares about. Remember—he hates us. His target is Christ. It has always been so since the beginning. His strategy is to wound Christ by abducting us. His plans for our demise are deliberate and consistent. They include:

• Twisting the truth so that his words and the Master's words will appear to be one and the same.

During the years when my sister and I were struggling to prove to each other that we were super spiritual because we were doing such good things in God's kingdom, we were lacking understanding about one critical point of spiritual growth. We didn't fully comprehend that we are saved by grace. We didn't know the formula: God+Nothing=Everything. So when the Impostor twisted down our throats his formula: Faith - Our Works = Dead Faith; we swallowed it hook, line, and sinker. Faith without works, according to James 2:20 is dead faith. But what the Impostor left out of his equation is only faith that is fueled by the power of the Master can produce good works.

The proof of our faith is that Christ does His work in us. Because we can do nothing to merit Christ's love, the formula for faith: God in us = good works, is not contrary to the formula for grace: God

+ Nothing = Everything. We can do nothing on our own, but in Christ we can do all things. A few word changes by the Impostor leads us to big misunderstandings about the Master. My sister and I have wonderful conversations today—no more competition—just very sweet fellowship.

• Creating chaos in our lives so we will be too busy to seek after the Master's heart.

After a hard day at work my husband said a quick hello and headed for the bedroom to take a nap. I was busy making dinner when the sounds of our children screaming, a barking dog, and a howling cat seemed to be headed my way. Before there was time to investigate, the commotion reached the kitchen. First the cat holding our hamster in her mouth streaked through the doorway with our dog running to catch the cat and the kids trying to catch the dog. I screamed. Then the processional circled through the family room and reversed their direction, only this time I was behind the cat, the dog was behind me, and the kids were still screaming. Trying to save the hamster, I yanked on the cat's tail just as the cat began to head upstairs. With her fur between my fingers, the cat yelled loudly, releasing the hamster, which was now bouncing down the stairs like a rubber ball. I caught the hamster. After the dust settled back into the carpet, Bud came stumbling out of the bedroom, took the hamster out of my hand, returned it to its cage, and went back to bed mumbling, "All I wanted to do was take a nap."

The Impostor knows that no one really gets to do what he or she needs to do when chaos is controlling our lives. When chaos reigns we have little time to truly seek the Master's heart. Quick prayers for help and sporadic times of seeking council are about all we can hope for. The difference between chaos and crisis is that in chaos everything gets stirred but nothing gets cooked. In crisis God remains able to lead us, quiet us on the inside, and turn all our adversities into reasons for praise.

• Causing a crisis of belief so we will question the Master's love for us.

Charlotte was a feisty and energetic business-woman who was brought to Portland from another state to manage the company I was working for. She and I became fast friends and great coworkers. Just three years after her arrival, however, the company was sold and Charlotte found herself in a new state with no job and heavy financial burdens to carry. For months she questioned God's love for her. "Why is God doing this to me?" was the constant cry of her heart. Any answer I could find to give her seemed to reach a dead end. Charlotte was in the middle of a stormy crisis of belief. As the waves of hurt and humiliation rolled over her, she remained so focused on the pain of her crisis that she continuously failed to see God as her lifeline in the midst of the turmoil.

Once the Impostor has the chance to convince us that God is doing awful things to us, he knows that we will not be able to grasp hold of the truth that will pull us through to safety. God never does things *to* us, He only wants to do things *through* us.

•Rendering us useless in the kingdom plan of the Master so we will not fulfill the Master's design for our lives.

Kathy was a young Christian wife and mother who was married to a non-Christian husband. Though her husband never voiced objections to her Christianity, Kathy seldom attended worship services and her children rarely came to church. When asked why she stayed home on Sunday mornings her answer was always the same. "I am waiting for my husband to come to church with me." As a result, this beautiful and talented woman never discovered the joy that comes from discovering God's plan for her life. She never found out how valuable she is to the body of Christ. Her children lost precious years of being in Sunday school, building healthy Christian friendships, memorizing Bible verses, and singing praises to God with other children. God loved Kathy, but Kathy's love for God never had a chance to shine through her life and in her home. Kathy was saved and stuck, and the Impostor was only too willing to keep her feet lodged in dry cement. Who knows how many people her faith might have touched or how many lives her children might have affected had their love for Jesus been encouraged to grow. Maybe her husband would have seen his need for Jesus through his children's childlike trust. The Impostor knows that though grace is free it isn't cheap. Our refusal to respond to God's grace by walking closely with Him will have far reaching effects on everyone we come in contact with. A useless Christian is a dangerous obstacle for others who need to know the Master.

•Satisfying us with earthly pleasures so we will not hunger for heavenly rewards.

Bud and I have a sailboat named the *Sensuous Sea*. Though the name raises the eyebrows of more than a few Christians who think the word *sensuous* is sinful, we nonetheless sport her through the water— name and all—whenever we get the chance. We chose the name because it expresses how we feel when we're on the water. Everything about sailing excites us. The smell of the wind, the sound of the waves, the quietness of mornings on the river, all pique our senses and fill us with great pleasure. We can be stressed to the max, but as soon as we climb on board our boat we forget everything that ails us. It's a good thing. But when our love for sailing pre-empts our love for the God who has blessed us with the boat and the water it floats on, we become the invited guests on the Impostor's yacht.

I don't believe it's the pleasures of life that trip us up as much as it is our satisfaction with them. Earthly pleasures were never intended to be the chief end of our pursuits. Instead, they are to be the aroma of God's goodness that draws us closer to Him. Any pleasure that doesn't lead to praise, the Impostor will use to keep us from praising his enemy. The Impostor knows that the more he can heighten our senses with empty pleasure the more addicted to pleasure we will become, and when we are hooked on the good feelings that pleasure produces we will seek his kind of pleasure instead.

HEEDING THE CALL TO REBELLION

My heart was smitten that day in the doctor's office as the transparency of the unborn baby was laid over the picture of the mother's womb. It was a portrait of total trust and harmony. The mother gave herself fully to her child and the child nestled comfortably in its mother's body. If my heart were photocopied on a clear piece of plastic and laid over a picture of my heavenly Father's heart, I wonder if my heart would fit as perfectly in Him as that baby fit inside its mother.

That peaceful picture may not sound like rebellion to you, but I believe it is. It is the kind of rebellion that defies the heart of the Impostor. It is the kind of rebellion that makes the Impostor the loser in my life. It is the kind of rebellion that causes my soul to be at rest and fully satisfied serving and loving one Master.

One day as I was leaving church, I saw a young woman that I hadn't seen in almost two years. With great excitement I ran up to her, wrapped my arms around her neck, and babbled on with a zillion words of greetings. When I finally took a moment to breathe, I noticed that her face was wet with tears. "Jill," I exclaimed, "what's wrong?"

"You haven't heard, have you?" she replied. "My baby died." With a picture of her precious cherub in her hand, she proceeded to fill me in on the details of her story.

After she and her husband settled into their new home, Jill gave birth to a beautiful daughter. Their family was almost perfect—a new home, two children, and a great future ahead of them. A few months later their baby began to grow weaker instead of stronger. Following weeks of tests, the prognosis was grim. Their baby had a terminal disease and would most likely die a slow and painful death. While Jill nursed her baby through the devastating illness she discovered that she was pregnant. The joy, however, was not to last. Jill miscarried the baby, and shortly afterward their daughter died.

I held Jill in my arms and wept with her. Then she looked into my eyes and said, "Sandy, how do I make sense of this? How do I find God in this? Where is His love?" Never have I been at such a loss for words. I silently called out to God for the words she needed to comfort her broken heart.

"Jill, do you see this picture of you and your baby? Notice the way you are holding your hurting child on your lap. Do you see the love in your face as you look down at her? Was there anything you wouldn't do to comfort her, or love her, or help her get through all those painful moments? Jill, do you think you can crawl into your heavenly Father's lap with all the pain you feel right now and let Him love you the way you loved your daughter?"

After a time of quiet reflection, Jill responded. "Sandy, I remember in our Bible study one time when you talked about what it meant to come home to the Father's heart. I didn't know what that meant at the time. Maybe now I do. Please pray for me. I need to find God's heart in all of this." Without knowing it, Jill was standing at the threshold of rebellion. She was entering the heavenly army of those whose hearts fit perfectly into the Father's heart. She was choosing who would be her Master.

It is when we curl up into the Father's heart that we deal

the fiercest deathblow to the Impostor. The Impostor has many ways of stealing what belongs to the Master. If pleasure doesn't work, he will use pain. His tools are many but his purpose is always the same—to keep our hearts from beating in sync with the heart of the Master.

We cannot serve two masters. If we want to have a single-hearted love for the authentic One we must identify His enemy and ours, face him squarely, and declare with uncompromising resolve, *No more!* It is only when we surrender all that we are to the Master that we will be able to recognize and resist the schemes of the Impostor. It is only when we give our hearts fully to Christ that we will be free to experience how truly significant we are. I invite you to join me in a new kind of rebellion. I invite you to hear and respond to the Master's voice as He calls to us, "Come back to My heart and follow Me."

Lord, you know
I'm such a stupid sheep.
I worry
About all sorts of things
Whether I'll find grazing land
Still cool water
A fold at night
In which I can feel safe.
I don't.
I only find troubles
want
loss.
I turn aside from You
To plan my rebel way.

I go astray.
I follow other shepherds
Even other stupid sheep.
Then when I end up
On some dark mountain
Cliffs before
Wild animals behind
I start to bleat
Shepherd, Shepherd,
Find me save me
Or I die,
And you do.[1]

A Heart in Training

The power is God's
but the vigilance is ours.

JACK HAYFORD, *MOMENTS WITH MAJESTY*

CHAPTER THREE

*B*ud and I love to sail. When the water is calm and the wind is stable, sailing is a profoundly rich experience. But there are times when the water turns evil, and the wind chases after you with harmful intent.

One day, while on our way to Astoria near the mouth of the Columbia River, a sea condition known as *widow makers* interrupted our peaceful voyage. We steadied ourselves for a bumpy ride as large waves rolled rapidly toward our boat. Then through the sounds of howling wind and splashing water, Bud heard a noise that appeared to be coming from the bow. Straining to see forward he discovered that our anchor had become dislodged from the pulpit and was banging sharply against the hull. In a rush of panic, my normally hyper-cautious husband raced forward to retrieve the anchor, wearing neither a life jacket nor a lifeline. With the tiller in my hand, my focus was drawn toward my husband as the widow makers crashed over him with relentless speed. Just as Bud was finally able to get a firm grip on the anchor, a gust of wind spun us out of control. Terror raged through me. Before I could scream, I heard him shouting through the storm, "Get back on course. Point her toward the marker."

Shifting my focus from my husband to the marker was

the most difficult order I have ever had to obey; nevertheless, I followed his command. After Bud fastened the anchor into its holder, we were once again headed in the right direction. We learned several lessons that day that have helped us to become better sailors when the seas put us to the test.

Danger also lurks around every corner for the woman who has surrendered her heart to the Master. As she turns her back on the Impostor and sets her focus on the course the Captain of her soul has charted for her, she can be sure that the winds of adversity will threaten her. Unless she is willing to study the charts and follow the rules, observe the conditions, trust the Captain, and steady the course, she might just end up in the water.

Before Bud and I purchased our first sailboat, we thought we were well on the road to becoming sailors. Bud, the one who always reads the directions first, bought every book he could find on sailing. Then he sat down and diligently read through each one until his head was so full of knowledge, he could throw nautical terms around like an expert. Yet, in spite of his intellectual acuity for our newfound sport, when it came to actually getting our boat out in the river with the sails up, we were still just bungling beginners. After we were handed the keys to our vessel, we realized the only thing we knew about sailing was how to get into the boat.

After three weeks of piloting our boat around the Portland area of the Columbia River, using just the engine, we decided we were finally ready to put up the sails. We did everything right—at first. We pointed the bow into the wind and shut off the engine. I manned the tiller, keeping her steady, while Bud hoisted up the sails. Then, with the sails secure, we waited for the wind to blow us to the other side of the river. However, during the time it took us to get the sails in position, we failed to notice that a fleet of sailboats was racing toward us. If there was wind in the air it certainly wasn't filling *our* sails because while the other boats were moving with frightening speed, we just sat there like a defenseless target. Within moments, two of the boats were nearly on top of us. Bud yelled out to them, "Go around us! We're new at this. We don't know what we're doing!" I covered my eyes and prayed out loud, "Oh, Jesus, oh, Jesus, get us out of this." The boats went around us. After the crisis had passed, I said to Bud, "Honey, would it have helped if we had turned the engine back on?"

Buying a boat doesn't make you a sailor—learning how to sail does. Are you tired of being tossed about through life's storms? Do you long for consistency in your walk with Christ? Is the yo-yo approach to spiritual growth leaving you weary and discouraged? Do you want to have the kind of faith that doesn't waver when the world around you is spinning out of control? Faith is more than a possession; it is a progression. It grows the more it is trained, tested, and trusted.

The faith I have was given to me as a gift from the Master so I could respond to Him when He offered me eternal life. When He chose me to be His child, He gave me all that I needed so that I could surrender my heart to Him. John Piper in his book *Future Grace* explained it with these words: "Faith is indeed the channel through which divine power and transformation flow to the soul; and the work of God through faith does indeed touch the soul, and change it."[1]

Though I may want to learn how to live according to the pattern given to us through Jesus Christ, my initial deposit of faith will not grow to maturity unless I choose to nurture and train this faith. Though nothing was required of me in the cancellation of my sin or the purchase of my place in heaven, something is required of me in the process of transforming how I live today into how God wants me to live tomorrow. Faith that is exercised through purposeful, careful training will produce more faith, stronger faith, and enduring faith.

Faith asks:
Who has promised?
Faith looks back:
to mercies given
to promises fulfilled
to victories won
Faith looks forward:
to new songs of deliverance
to new wells of understanding
to new reasons for rejoicing
Faith fills:
the past with gratitude
the present with peace
and the future with hope
Faith finishes:
the course with belief
that what was said in the beginning
has been made perfect in the end.

SANDY SNAVELY 1997

I know what it's like to bounce back and forth between faith and unfaith. My early walk with Christ consisted of a few spiritual highs joined together by many spiritual lows. A good sermon would send my spirit soaring. Then a small trial would hurl my confidence to the ground. A retreat would put me on top of the mountain, but coming home to catsup on the floor and rat's nests in my children's hair would toss me into the valley of discouragement. I longed to be like the women in my church who seemed to float through life with the grace of a butterfly in spring. My failure to achieve the gracefulness they personified wasn't due to my lack of desire. I failed because I wanted the results of their maturity without applying myself to the disciplines that were necessary to get me there. Visualization of a goal is a poor substitute for training.

Oswald Chambers put it this way: "You did not do anything to achieve your salvation, but you must do something to exhibit it."[2]

Sin is a difficult enemy to constrain. All the things that thrill the Impostor and wound the heart of the Master sprout effortlessly from our flesh. We never have to teach ourselves to be bitter or angry or shallow. Growing slack in our responsibilities comes naturally to us. Forgetting to love others is simple to do when our hearts are vulnerable and needy. Spiteful words fire rapidly off our tongues when we feel our rights have been violated. Sin comes easily to us.

Spiritual growth doesn't happen overnight. You won't get it by hearing a good speaker. It won't rub off on you by sitting next to it in a worship service. Without careful training, sin will seek to strangle our faith so that we will be unable to develop a healthy, consistent, and mature walk with Christ. In other words, if we want real change in our lives, we need to apply ourselves to becoming grown-ups in Christ.

When I was a child, I talked like a child, I thought like
a child, I reasoned like a child. When I became a [woman],
I put childish ways behind me. (1 Corinthians 13:11)

FROM INFANCY TO MATURITY

Some people who want to learn how to sail, start off with a small boat first so they can see whether or not sailing is what they really want to do. Not so for Bud and me—we started right off with a twenty-two-foot boat and a rented spot at a local moorage. Our first trek down the ramp at Cliff's Marina was a ghostly experience. As we made our way to our boat we passed by several other boats which had not been out of their slips in so long that small trees were literally growing through their hulls. It was hard to fathom why people would pay rent every month for a place to harbor boats that were never used. We understood this better after we experienced firsthand how hard sailing can be when you don't know what you are doing.

I have known far too many Christians who, after years of knowing Christ as their Savior, still sit in their slips with algae-covered hearts because they are afraid the Christian life is just too hard for them to live. Filled with a fear of failure, reluctant to give up their old ways of living, uninspired by biblical teaching, and just not convinced that they need more of Christ, they stash their ticket to heaven in their back pockets and go on about their business. At some point in their growth they lost sight of the price that was paid for them to sit idle and become stagnant in the Master's kingdom.

The most important thing Bud and I had going for us in our early days of sailing was a strong desire not only to learn to sail, but to learn to sail well. We wanted to become seasoned sailors. After weeks of providing hilarious moments of comic relief to our neighbors at the moorage, we began to understand four of the most important principles that every sailor needs to know. First, if you want to be safe in the water you absolutely *must* study the charts and follow rules. Second, you *must* learn to observe the conditions around you. Third, you absolutely *must* trust your captain. And fourth, you *must* keep on a steady course. These four *musts* are not optional. They are not good suggestions. They are the unshakable, unmovable rules of the road that keep us safe no matter what obstacles may come our way.

I know many fine Christians today are troubled by the word *must*. Yet, if we truly want to grow in Christ, there are some things that we really must do. The word *must* is a part of the natural laws of life. If we want to live we must breathe. If we want to grow, we must eat. If we want to see where we are going, we must keep our eyes open. If we want to grow in Christ, we must apply our hearts to those things that will help us reach our objectives. There are many *musts* in the word of God, and all of them are written for our good. They are God's gracious guideposts to keep us on track with Him.

1. Study the Charts and Follow the Rules

Just after Bud and I tied up our boat at a dock in Washington, we stopped to watch a powerboat that was coming in our direction. As it raced toward a slip near us, we noticed it was headed dangerously close to the boat that was docked next to the place they were aiming for. The guy driving the boat yanked on the wheel and missed the back of the other boat by a hair. His near miss, however, caused him to hit the corner of the dock instead. A few more tugs at the wheel and he was now scraping and bumping against his side of the dock. Then his friend jumped out of the boat onto the dock and proceeded to direct him into their slip. Once the boat was in position, the guy on the dock yelled, "You've got it. She's perfect." Perfect?

I wondered what he thought mediocre would have looked like. In just a few minutes these two yahoos had managed to break every rule in the book. They didn't cut their speed, they didn't have their lines ready, they weren't wearing life jackets, and they didn't put their beer cans down while docking their boat. These guys were dangerous.

News reports of capsized boats are common in Oregon. The Columbia River has the reputation of being one of the most difficult rivers in the country to navigate. Strong currents, sandbars, and tree trunks floating in the water only add to the risk of running into trouble. Many of our ocean ports have narrow inlets that make getting in and out treacherous for even the most seasoned sailors. Many of the reported tragedies could have been averted had the people in charge of their boats taken the time to prepare themselves for the worst of what could happen. It's been my experience that the only people who hate rules are the ones who haven't had their lives saved by them.

The purpose of God's Word is to build wise people and censor fools. The Word of God is not just a book of rules, it's a road map that leads us to the Master. It's a picture of the Father's heart and His love for His creation. It's an open door to heaven. The Word of God is the most perfect piece of literature ever written and the most accurate account of man's beginnings ever found. It is deep enough to challenge the most brilliant people and simple enough for me to understand. It is able to feed a hungry soul, make blind eyes see, and give life to dead people. It can pierce through a hardened heart and heal a broken one. The Word of God was so vital to Moses that in his parting address to Israel he warned them, "'Take to heart all the words I have solemnly declared to you this day, so that you may command your children to obey carefully all the words of this law. They are not just idle words for you—they are your life'" (Deuteronomy 32:46–47a).

I love mornings. With a cup of tea by my side and an afghan across my lap, I sit alone with God ready to let Him serve me breakfast from His word. These quiet times have become food and nourishment for my life. However, the pleasantness of the picture I have just painted for you has not always been the case for me and for my devotional life. I have had times of drought when spending time in the Word seemed as profitable as drinking sand on a hot day. There have been times when I have purposely avoided opening up the Bible so I could protect my own willfulness from the conviction of God's commands. I have been guilty of using my time in the Word as a tool to help me prove to others how brilliant I am.

Looking back on those times, it is easy to see why I struggled against spending time studying the Word of God. I saw my time as a chore. I thought God would be mad at me and withhold blessings from me if I didn't open up His book. The wonderful thing about those times was that though I didn't have the right attitude and motivation for "doing my devotions" God was still able to speak to my heart and eventually correct my misconceptions. Over the course of time, the Word has not returned to me void. Though sometimes hot and sometimes cold, my love affair with God's Word has continued to grow. The more I spend time in it the more time I want to spend because God has chosen to use those special times to show Himself to me.

"Come, all you who are thirsty,
come to the waters;
and you who have no money,
come, buy and eat!
Come, buy wine and milk
without money and without cost....
For my thoughts are not your thoughts,
neither are your ways my ways," declares the LORD.
"As the heavens are higher than the earth,
so are my ways higher than your ways
and my thoughts than your thoughts."

ISAIAH 55:1, 8–9

If you are one who struggles in developing a consistent and fruitful quiet time with God, be encouraged. You are still a deeply loved child of the Master. The Impostor loves complacency, fatigue, insecurity, stubbornness, pride, and busy schedules. But if the Impostor thought for one moment that the Master didn't care to spend *His* time with *you,* he would not think twice about interfering with your desire to study the charts so that you will know how to follow the rules.

God wants to spend quality time with us. His heart longs to commune with us. There are so many things He wants to tell us. He has seen the way we get so easily flustered by life's challenges, and He has insights and answers that will help get us through the hard times. There are principles waiting to be shared with us if only we will come and let Him speak. He loves the joy we have when we learn new things about Him. He treasures our sorrow when we find that we have failed to live up to His standards. He desires to lift us up out of the pit, dust us off, and help us to start all over again. He loves our time with Him.

I still have times in my life when I don't quite feel like giving up a portion of my day to open the door to His visits. Perhaps the reason I sometimes shy away from meeting Him through His word is because I forget that when I sit down with Him I am spending time with the kindest, wisest person I've ever known. Instead, I think that maybe my quiet times are all about me and my busy schedule or my silly inferiority. I still tend to forget that God is not waiting to judge me or hurt me; He just wants to love me and help me grow. When I am prepared to have His presence transform me a little bit each time I open His book, I end up feeling encouraged by His wonderful patience with me—His growing child. When I see God's patience with me as I learn how to live the Christian life, I find that I am able to be patient with myself and surrender who I am to the power of God's Word at work in me.

We *must* not wait for our feelings to provoke us to action. We *must* not allow our schedules to rule our decision to study the charts so that we can follow the rules. If we wait for a better time to come—it won't. Consistent time in the Word is repugnant to the Impostor and counterproductive to his designs for your time; therefore, our rebellion against him will be marked by our firm decision to be *intentional* about our growth.

> *"Let not the wise [woman] boast of [her] wisdom*
> *or the strong [woman] boast of [her] strength.*
> *or the rich [woman] boast of [her] riches,*
> *but let [her] who boasts boast about this:*
> *that [she] understands and knows me,*
> *that I am the LORD, who exercises kindness,*

> *justice and righteousness on earth,*
> *for in these I delight," declares the LORD.*
>
> JEREMIAH 9:23–24

2. Observe the Conditions

We were having a peaceful day on the river. The sun was up; there was a quiet breeze that was just enough to fill our sails and move us gently through the water. Then Bud noticed some little cat's paws swirling on top of the water. Cat's paws are like the fingerprints of the air telling you that the wind is coming. We looked up and saw the clouds growing darker by the minute. We could smell rain. A storm was on its way. The time spent studying the charts and learning to follow the rules prepared us for what needed to be done. We took down the sails and headed for shelter. Because we knew the right things about sailing, we were able to observe the conditions around us and put what we knew into practice.

We must have our senses well tuned to the world around us if we are going to be able to apply what we *know* to what we *see*. Meditation on God's Word helps us to do that. Meditation is the contemplative reflection that weaves what we know into what we see. It never works apart from truth. It rehearses what has already been studied and makes it personal. Meditation takes the simple ordinary things of life and teaches us intimate lessons of who God is and how He cares for us.

Nineteen ninety-eight was a very difficult year for our family. Just before the year began, my twenty-year-old nephew was killed in a car accident. Then, one week later, my mother had a severe stroke. She died shortly after New Year's Day. My mother-in-law moved into our home as the year was ending, and then just before Christmas she went home to be with the Lord. So many of my dear friends expressed loving sadness for the year that smelled of death. Yet, as tragic as 1998 had been, it was a wonderful year to contemplate life and the God who created it.

One evening as I sat holding my mother-in-law's hand, watching her breathe, and wondering if each breath she took would be her last, God revealed a tender look at life to me. I thought back to how life begins. The first thing a mother has to give her child is love. For nine months there is little else she can do for her baby but love it. Then the baby is born, with no dignity, and no way of caring for itself. So, with great love and compassion the mother nourishes and cleans the child until the child can do those simple tasks on its own. Then the mother counts all of her baby's firsts. Its first bite of solid food. Its first giggle. Its first time sitting up without help. Its first word and its first step. As the child grows it learns to do almost everything on its own until after a time it needs almost nothing from its mother but love. Then time passes, and the child grows old. Little by little she gives up the dignity she gained through all her years of learning how to be self-reliant. Again she needs to be cared for, and someone else begins to count not her firsts, but her lasts. Her last trip down the hall. Her last look at the Christmas tree. Her last taste of solid food. Her last time sitting up on her own. Her last word. And soon her last breath. While holding Mom's precious, tiny hand, I realized all I could now do for my mother-in-law was to love her. Life had come full circle.

Although my mother-in-law is gone, I have gained a view of life that will live with me as I prepare to follow her path through my aging years. And God, the Alpha and the Omega, the beginning and the end, the One who began my life by loving me, will love me till the end. His Word has taught me that wonderful truth, yet meditation has shown it to me.

Meditation keeps our minds occupied with eternal thoughts so we will be able to stand against the lies of the Impostor. When he says that life is all there is, contemplating the wonder of life exposes his twisted ideas. Meditation is also a springboard to obedience. When I think God's *musts* are just too hard to do, contemplation of what He has done in the past keeps me on track. Richard Foster defines it in these words: "Christian meditation, very simply, is the ability to hear God's voice and obey His word."[3]

When I watch the waves roll onto the shore, meditation reminds me that God has put a boundary on where they should stop. When trials roll over the shores of my life this living picture illustrates for me that they will not be allowed to cross beyond the boundaries of the One who stands guard over my circumstances. (*See* Job 38:8–11.)

When I wipe the sand off my feet, God whispers to me that His thoughts of me far outnumber the millions of little granules that I am brushing away. I am never alone. I am never even a moment's time away from the mind of my heavenly Father. (*See* Psalm 139:17–18.)

When I squint my eyes to diffuse the brightness of the sun, I am reminded that the paths of the righteous will continue to grow brighter and brighter just like the noonday sun. Though my path of life may seem dim or complex, I know the way will become clearer in time as I walk it in faith with the One who knows the end as well as He knows the beginning. (*See* Proverbs 4:18.)

The regular practice of meditation helps us to see what

God has already told us that He is. As we open our spiritual eyes and look around us we see the colors of the earth and know that He is the Creator. We see how diligently a sparrow cares for her young, and we are reminded of how God is caring for us. We watch the sun come up on a new day, no matter what we did the day before, and we can see that God is forgiving. We see how a rose bush survived the winter and we know that God is competent.

Meditation teaches us new habits of godliness as we discover the character of God reflected in all we see, hear, think, and do. Meditating upon the Word keeps us near to the heart of the Master and gives us a biblical perspective from which to view life.

> But [her] delight is in the law of the LORD,
> and on his law [she] meditates day and night.
> [She] is like a tree planted by streams of water,
> which yields its fruit in season
> and whose leaf does not wither.
> Whatever [she] does prospers.
>
> PSALM 1:2–3

3. Trust the Captain

> I love the LORD, for he heard my voice;
> he heard my cry for mercy.
> Because he turned his ear to me,
> I will call on him as long as I live.
>
> PSALM 116:1–2

During the storm where the widow makers nearly washed my husband overboard, my trust in Bud as the captain was put to the crucial test. When he told me to stop looking at him and focus back on the marker, I had to be absolutely sure that he was right before I could obey his command. Yet, because I knew him so well and because I had seen him get us out of so many other predicaments, I knew that I could trust his wisdom and do what he told me to do. Because I have an intimate friendship with my captain, I am able to trust him when the weather gets rough.

Intimacy cannot be developed without close, open, and transparent communication. Prayer is the process of getting to know the Master on an intimate level through honest, heart-exposed conversation. The more intimate we become with our heavenly Father the more we discover how unquestionably trustworthy He is.

Have you ever considered how astounding it is that we can actually come into the presence of a holy God and live to talk about it? The God who created all things, the One who holds the keys to life and death in His hands has given us permission to approach His throne and speak intimately with Him. Jesus made this possible when He died on the cross and the curtain that separated God from His people was torn in two.

If you could picture with me for a moment what it used to be like for the Hebrews to approach God before Jesus came. Moses instructed his people to build a tabernacle according to the exact design given to him by God on Mount Sinai. The design of the tabernacle was a blueprint for how God's children were to come to Him. Anyone could enter the outer courtyards, but only the priests could perform the duties of preparing the way to God. Just after the entry gate stood a brazen altar where the priests would receive a living sacrifice as a symbol of the people's admission of sin. After the brazen altar, a large basin provided a means for cleansing the priests who had performed the sacrifice. Then when the priests had been cleansed, they were able to enter the first holy place. They would pass through three items of great significance—the Bread of Presence, the Lampstand, and the Altar of Incense. A thick veil separated the Holy Place from the Most Holy Place. Only the high priest of Israel could enter the Most Holy Place, and that was only once a year. This place was so holy that the robe worn by the high priest had little bells on the edge of it so that the priests waiting outside would know whether or not the high priest was alive inside. Only one piece of furniture was placed inside this Most Holy Place—the Ark of Promise. Inside the ark was the evidences of God's faithfulness to His people: a sample of the manna which God sent to feed His people in the wilderness, Aaron's (the first high priest) rod which had budded as a sign of God's endorsement of his leadership, and the tablets that contained the Ten Commandments. The Most Holy Place was most holy because the Most Holy God dwelt there. It was an awesome and terrifying thing to approach the presence of the living God.

In contrast today, all we have to do is call upon God's name. Moreover, the Most Holy Place dwells right inside the heart of every believer. This privilege has not been granted to us because we are better than the Hebrews who lived during Old Testament times. It is rather that Jesus, who was the sacrifice for our sin, has given us the right to walk with Him into the presence of His Father. Correspondingly, He is the Bread of Life (Bread of Presence), the Light of the World (Lampstand) that leads us to His Father, and He prays for us

continuously before the Father's throne (the Altar of Incense).
When He died on the cross, the veil in the temple was torn
in two giving us access to the Most Holy Place where the Most
Holy God dwells. Thus, it is no small thing that because of
Jesus, God has given us permission to come and sit with Him,
to know Him intimately, and to receive His mercy.

Prayer is a two-way conversation with God. Over the
years prayer has joined my heart and God's heart together in
close, intimate fellowship. As He writes the chapters of my
life's story, prayer weaves the themes together charting
progress, defining failure, and making course corrections
along the way. There is much unseen activity that takes place
while I am praying. When I don't know how to pray—the
Holy Spirit groans in prayer for me (Romans 8:26). When I
am embarrassed because of my sin—Jesus intercedes for me
(Romans 8:34; 1 Timothy 2:5; Hebrews 7:25). When the
holiness of God overwhelms me—He leads me to His throne
and assures me that I am free to approach Him without fear
(Hebrews 4:16). When I think my prayers are only meaningless chatter—I find in the book of Revelation a picture of the
four living creatures and the twenty-four elders holding the
prayers of the saints in golden bowls of incense. I am humbled to know that my prayers are so well cared for in heaven
(Revelation 5:8). When I feel as if my prayers are spinning
aimlessly around the room—I need only to be reminded by
these verses that I am not alone when I pray, and what I say
matters to God.

Prayer is speaking to God. Prayer is pleading with God.
Prayer is chatting with God over the events of the day. Prayer
is seeing God as your best friend, your only hope, your mirror, your confidante, your source of wisdom and strength,

your salvation, and your joy. Prayer is a continual feast of fellowship with the Sovereign Lord of the universe.

In order for the feast to begin, we need to plan on not only speaking to this great God, but we need to learn how to listen as He speaks to us. Just as there is structure to any meaningful conversation, there is structure to prayer. Some of the characteristics of this structure include praise, confession, requests, and thanksgiving. More than a formula, prayer is a relationship built on love, honesty, transparency, and a great longing to be near God's throne where grace and mercy wait for us.

The more we desire to spend time with the Master, the more the Impostor will wave the hands of time in front of us. His clock ticks loudly, reminding us of how little time is left to complete our earthly tasks. But eternity has no clock. It never takes time away from us—instead, it fulfills time in us. It was in the fullness of time that God sent His Son to be our Savior—now we have the fullness of Him in return for our time.

O, Fullness of Time,
fill my time
until the time
when the ticking of it
spills into eternity
and flows into the sea of timelessness
where the hands of time
can never again draw my heart
away from You.

SANDY SNAVELY 1997

4. *Steady the Course*

We didn't know there was fog ahead. When Bud and I left the moorage in Cathlamet and headed the *Sensuous Sea* out into the Columbia River, a thick cloud of fog enveloped our boat. Within moments we could barely see two feet in any direction. We tried to make our way toward where we thought our next marker would be, but our efforts were useless. Bud chose to use our instruments to trace our way back to where we started so we could chart our course along the shoreline. His strategy worked and once again we were safe. Danger was averted on the Columbia.

Though our vision was darkened for a while, we found that nothing had changed once the sun began to shine through the mist. There are times in our lives that we can't always see our way clearly. Answers to critical life decisions may not appear magically before us. Storms may throw us off course for a while, and we might feel like we will never be able to find our way back to where we know God wants us to be. This is why we *must* apply ourselves to these four vital principles of growth. Our time alone with God in study, meditation, and prayer provides us with the wisdom needed to stay on course. They are our instruments through which the Holy Spirit is able to point us in the direction that we need to go. When we stray off course they bring us back to our marker so we can once again steady the course to home.

Danger lies ahead. The Impostor is waiting to entice us away from the Master. Strange philosophies dressed in spirituality are seeking to devour our understanding of God. Opportunities will spread before us that will offer an easier way to reach our destination. Fearful thoughts will attempt to take our mind captive. Discouragement will hover over us to swallow up our joy. Seasons of dryness will test our endurance. Detour signs will tempt us to go off course.

There is a distinct difference between the woman who makes herself the focus of her own attention and the woman who allows God to become the center of her life. One searches for self-fulfillment, finding instead a superficial peace that can be blown away by the slightest puff of adversity. The other seeks to know her God. This process of knowing God produces the evidence of a changed life that will withstand the hurricanes of life's unmerciful crises. She will look into her mirror and see the reflection of an approved character. She will open her hands and find that the results of her efforts have constructed lasting results. She will trace the steps of her life and see that she has chosen the right course and know that she has been perfectly led by the God who chose her to be His daughter.

We, as the Master's children, have not been called to follow a course that has no destination. The course we are on is the course that will lead us to heaven. Some will be satisfied to stumble through the gates of heaven with just a fist full of understanding of how they got there, others will sail into heaven's shores waving their charts and shouting, "I'm here! I read the charts and followed the rules as best as I could. I observed the conditions and I saw God everywhere—it was glorious. I trusted the Captain and everything He told me to do was right. And I steadied the course through all the storms and now I'm here. Thank you, Jesus."

The day will come when the earthly remains of our lives will be packed away in the dust of the ground. A stone will be placed as a commentary of the lives we lived on this mortal soil. What will be inscribed on our stones? If God were to

write our epitaphs, I wonder what He would say as the summation of our existence. My heart's desire is that He would
inscribe into the gravestone of my life, these words:

> *This stone is a remembrance of my daughter Sandy—*
> *may those who loved her be comforted,*
> *I was delighted to take her home because*
> *she delighted herself in Me!*

Having believed the Master's words until the end, I
hope to close my eyes on the world I have known and open
them to the bright Light of heaven, and maybe if there is
time, my last word on earth will be my first word in par-
adise, "Look!"

We live in demanding times. Much is expected of us as
wives, mothers, friends, neighbors, churchwomen, working
women, and more. Without a clear view of God and a deep
understanding of who we are in Him and what He has called
us to do, I don't see how it is possible for us to stand against
the lies of the Impostor. I invite you to come with me as we
seek to discover, from the Master's perspective, our true purpose as women in the areas of marriage, home, children,
friends, church, job, and our world. Remember the words of
Moses, "They are not just idle words for you—they are your
life" (Deuteronomy 32:47a). The only way to defeat the
Impostor is to turn our backs on him, turn our faces to the
Master, and do what He calls us to do. This is the rebellion
we have been called to; it is the key to a single-hearted love
for God.

THE CALL OF THE IMPOSTOR

Hear my voice dear woman. I know the needs of your heart. I am prepared to give you all that you deserve to have. I will not dictate to you what you should do or what you should be. I have the deepest respect for your choices. Built within you is a dream that must come to fruition. If you fail to accomplish this vision you will die from the wanting of it. I see that you are capable of doing so much more than even the Master has said you can do. You must be free to explore the world that is before you. Your significance is like a buried treasure waiting to be unearthed. Let me help you hold the shovel as we dig to discover it together. When you find the jewels that lie hidden within you, you will be ready to receive the praise that will be due you. You are a spiritual entity, with wisdom and knowledge that only a precious few have been fortunate to possess. Embrace your destiny. Fly with freedom to the prize of your calling. The Master will be more than pleased by your ability to accomplish good things for the world He has made, but you must find your place in this world. Listen to the voices that would help you to achieve all these things. They will come to you from many surprising sources. Doesn't the Master speak in many ways? Hear then all the counsel that is given to you, through people, music, books, trends, friends, and avoid the danger that will take you off course. That danger is the temptation to forsake the inner cravings of your soul that are your truest and purest self. It is to this unhealthy and narrow way that you must rebel. I am here to cheer you on. Now go forward and fulfill the mission that is before you. Go and find yourself, and may peace be with you as you do.

THE CALL OF THE MASTER

Hear me speak, dear child of mine. I formed you in your mother's womb. I know you more fully than your closest companion. Do you want your life to count for something in this world that I have made? Do you want to understand your identity and find your significance amidst the sea of faces that surround you? If this is what you desire then *know* this first of all—you will not find these things apart from Me. Come into My heart. You will see yourself as I see you, all that you have been, all that you are, and all that you will be—but I will not show you these things if you bring the world's philosophies with you. Let go of all that you are holding so tightly in your hands, then you will have room for the blessings that I have prepared for you. Set your focus on Me, and refuse all the vanities that will tempt you off course. It is when you have a clear view of Me that you will see Me and know My ways. My ways will be the guide for you to follow. Love, study, and treasure all that I have given you in My Word. You will be blessed beyond what you could ever have planned for yourself. Stand firmly against the Impostor's call. This is the rebellion that pleases Me, when you turn your back on all that is counterfeit and embrace the Truth. I love you with everlasting, eternal love. You are Mine. My arms are waiting to wrap themselves around you when you come bounding through My gates and we will at last see each other face to face. This, dear woman, is the prize to which I have called you. Now heed My call, resist the Impostor, stay the course, and I will give you all that you desire. Delight yourself in Me and I will bring it all to pass.

PART TWO

*Single-Hearted Life
in Christ*

The Heart that Says,
"I Do"

He made her for the man.
Then he made her from the man…flesh of his flesh,
bone of his bone, like and yet wondrously unlike.
Finally he brought her to the man,
designed exactly to suit his particular need,
prepared to meet that need for a helper and then,
in divine wisdom and love, given.

ELIZABETH ELLIOTT, *LOVE HAS A PRICE TAG*

It was a dreary November day and the day after President Kennedy had been assassinated when I met the man who was to become my husband. I always imagined that one day a tall, dark, and handsome man would meet me at the door and sweep me off my feet. But when the doorbell rang on that eventful Saturday evening, I stood before a young, medium, light, and pleasant Marine who was introduced to me as Bud Snavely. The date was set up through a friend who went to great lengths to convince me that Bud and I would be a really "cute couple." However, as I stood there giving him the once over, I knew that he was *not* my husky Italian dream man.

Ours did not appear to be a successful first date. Bud dashed my fantasies of romance the moment he began trying to top my jokes. He didn't like me either. After he had sacrificed his last few dollars to buy us burgers and shakes at our local A&W drive-in and the evening was over, we said a polite goodnight, each expecting not to see the other again, and I sent him away kissless. In spite of all this, two weeks later we went out on a second date. This time when Bud walked through the door, our eyes met and our hearts began to flutter. The man who was medium, light, and pleasant turned my fantasy around and captured my heart. Four months later we were married.

I fell in love with Bud because he was a person of quiet compassion and perceptive insight. He looked beyond my comedic mask and zeroed into my heart. Coming from a home of alcoholism and abuse, Bud's kindness made me feel protected and loved.

Within four years we became a family with two adorable children, Annette Marie and Dean Ellis, a little house in Portland, and a homeless dog named Sissy. All I ever hoped to have was right in front of me, and yet I was deeply miserable.

Through all my growing-up years I looked toward my future in terms of "I will be happy when..." *I will be happy when* I can make a lot of friends in school. Then, after working hard at building a long list of friends I stared into my happiness cup only to find that it was still empty. My next "I will be happy when" became *I will be happy when* I can excel in drama and speech. Through lots of hard work and determination, I became the apple of my drama teacher's eye, won almost every lead in every school play, and in my senior year I won first place in Humorous Interpretation at the California State Forensics Competitions. But my cup remained empty. As I neared the end of high school I set my sights on a new "I will be happy when." *I will be happy when* I find the man of my dreams, move away from home, and have children of my own. Then I met Bud. I found my man, moved out of state, and became a mother. Yet, with all my goals met, the cup that had been empty for so long remained dry. My "I will be happy when" turned into a sad resignation of "Maybe I won't be happy ever."

I had a vision of what marriage would be like, but the reality of our marriage rose nowhere near to the level of my expectations. Within a year after Bud and I exchanged our wedding vows, we didn't even give each other goose bumps anymore. He seldom came dancing through the door singing, *"Honey, I'm home."* We couldn't afford cozy dinners in candlelit restaurants. And, our conversations no longer went hours into the night. We ceased to astound each other with our wit and wisdom. We were becoming dull married people with dull married things to do: cleaning sinks, paying bills, pulling weeds, and a host of other tasks that neither of us found fun or romantic. Though I didn't know what marriage was supposed to look like, I was sure that ours had fallen far short of whatever the ideal was.

As a kid growing up in the early 60s, two-parent households were common. In spite of the countless married couples surrounding me, I still had no clear perspective on what caused marriages to succeed or fail. What I needed was to see marriage from a new perspective.

During my years as a radio broadcaster I discovered that a media pass has its privileges. A flash of my badge and I was escorted up to the press box, high above the crowds with a window that provided an expansive view of the arena below. Our radio listeners received full and accurate coverage of major events as they happened. A well-designed press box helps the press to see what others can't see from the bleachers below.

The woman who is *in* Christ has been invited by the Master to sit with Him in His press box so she can view all that He has created and can understand the purpose for which all things were made from His eternal perspective.

Marriage is a relationship that can only be clearly understood when viewed from the Master's position. From there we can see what marriage is not, what marriage is, and what we need to do to bring it into conformity with His perfect plan. There are many good books that give detailed instructions for *how* to build great marriages. What we need first, however, if we are to stand against the Impostor's plans to destroy the institution of marriage, is to have the Master's passion for His creation of matrimony. So, let's step up to the window and see if we can see marriage from the Master's heart.

WHAT MARRIAGE IS NOT

It was the most romantic evening a woman could hope for. Bud surprised me by picking me up from work and taking me to a little French restaurant near downtown Portland. Everything about that night was perfect, from the peach tablecloths to the fussy French waiters carrying white napkins over their left forearms. Overcome by the bliss of love, I can still remember staring into my husband's sweet face while resting my chin on my hand and thinking how perfect our evening together was. Bud's eyes returned a loving glance as he leaned in tenderly to my face and whispered ever so softly, "Sandy, you're drooling."

What a mood breaker!

Most couples get married because they feel better when they're together than they do when they're apart. When a marriage ends in divorce or emotional abandonment, it is an indication that something happened after the rings were exchanged that made being apart feel better than being together.

Feel-good moments in marriage are those enjoyable times in the day that make life with the one you love livable. Over the years my list of feel-good moments in marriage has grown to include:

- Hearing Bud laugh
- Feeling the warmth of his hand on mine when we go for walks together
- Hearing him say "I love you"
- The times when he stops reading the paper to listen to me talk
- Hearing his heartfelt apology for a wrong that has been done
- Sitting next to him at church, hearing him pray, watching him tear up during a schmultzy movie, sailing together, listening to him talk to our kids, watching him mow the lawn, hearing him say "be careful driving" when I head out the door.

Yet, as wonderful as those feel-good moments are, they are not the sum total of my life with Bud. Our marriage contains moments of romance, but it is held together by the decision we made many years ago to live together forever. However, although we have been married for over thirty-five years, our decision to be committed to each other was not made the night we were married. It came on the heels of near disaster. Had we not gained a new perspective on marriage from the Master's press box, our marriage would have been just another sad story of what happens when wedded bliss becomes matrimonial misery.

Marriage Is Not a Romance Novel

For the first ten years of our marriage Bud and I struggled to keep our act together. Though we earnestly loved each other, we had a difficult time living together. I was impulsive and high strung; Bud was steady and controlled. I wanted us to do everything together; he wanted regular times of being alone. When I felt optimistic; he felt pessimistic. I analyzed everything; he analyzed nothing. But then there were times when he would come through the door with a single rose in his hand and make all the bad times go away. Because of that, I thought our marriage would always be strong enough to survive our annoying idiosyncrasies.

One evening, however, shortly before our tenth anniversary, Bud changed the course of our pleasant conversation with these words: "Sandy, I want a divorce!" Within two weeks I watched my husband pack up his belongings and leave our home. When he left, I felt as if a piece of my heart had been torn from my flesh. Our marriage had ceased to feel the way it did when we first said, "I do," so when it seemed as if we were experiencing more love breakers than feel-good moments, Bud was ready to say, "I don't."

Our dreams of what marriage was supposed to be received their deathblow the day Bud announced that he was leaving me. What neither of us understood during those turbulent years was that we didn't have a clue as to what the real purpose of marriage was. We began our lives together in a murky sea of mistaken notions and childish fantasies. We thought that because we loved each other, being together as a married couple would always make us feel as good as we felt when we were dating. We each thought we had found the perfect someone who would love us beyond our flaws.

Moreover, I believe we thought we each found the one person in the world who had no flaws!

When we were crazy in love, all of our annoying habits seemed cute and even endearing. When Bud would change the subject in the middle of a conversation, I would giggle over his spontaneity. When I would bat my eyes and ask him to do something for me, his heart would melt and he'd trip over his own feet hurrying to get right on it. But after we were married and the honeymoon was far behind us, those cute little things became irritating, nagging love breakers.

Love breakers have a way of sneaking up on us after the honeymoon is over. They don't move in all at once; they just arrive one at a time until their numbers are powerful enough to snuff the joy out of otherwise happy relationships. Many marriages don't crumble because of big love breakers like adultery, alcoholism, or abuse. It's the accumulation of the little ones that finally crush them to death. While listening to many of our friends during those unhappy years grumble about their mates, I was able to formulate a sizeable list of marriage's most common love breakers. They include:

- Rudeness, lack of manners
- Sloppiness
- Sarcasm
- Laziness/Workaholism
- Selfishness, anger, bitterness, or a complaining spirit
- Broken promises
- Underspending/Overspending
- An expanding waist line, bad breath, sweaty hands, smelly feet, greasy hair.

This isn't what we expected marriage to be. A woman in search of the perfect romance will be bitterly disappointed when her hero rides home from work on his white charger, bounds through the door, walks past her, and flops into his recliner for a long evening nap.

Romance novels can be gratifying time wasters. They may even provide great moments of escape from the realities of life. The heroes in the stories are strong, lusty, and able to rescue their fair young maidens from distress. The maidens are beautiful, demure, and playful. Money flows from a never ending fountain and happy endings are always just a few chapters away.

The problem with romance novels is that most of them are myths. They lie to us about what love looks like and how marriage should be. The writers of their scripts paint the illusion that falling in love is just about being happy. But romance novels fail to illustrate the real reason why the Master created and loves marriage.

Marriage Is Not a Scepter

I love to paint. Painting is power. When I paint, I use my brush as a scepter, and I can turn my kingdom into anything I want it to be. My canvas is a willing subject in my quest for world domination. Just an unseemly piece of white cloth stretched over a wooden frame, it waits to be transformed into a work of art.

How easy marriage would be if husbands were willing subjects like our canvases. If Bud were a more willing subject, my dreams of endless romance would have been fulfilled by now. Bud, however, is not that compliant. Oh sure, he appears on the surface to be sweet, patient, and easygoing, but as soon as I give him even one simple suggestion that will help him to improve himself, he rebels. I can assume one of two things about this man I married. One, he is the most stubborn man I've ever met, or two, he just doesn't love me enough to accept my well-meaning suggestions. As the queen in my castle, whenever I have tried to zap my husband with my scepter of change, he just plants his feet and refuses to be reconfigured.

Before I recommitted my life to Christ, I used my scepter on my husband in an effort to eliminate all the love breaking habits I found to be so unbecoming. My ability to bark orders like a drill sergeant made us both feel surly. "Bud, can't you just pick up your socks? Is it too much to ask for you to empty the garbage? Why do you always have to wear that disgusting T-shirt?" Bud was not a fighter, so whenever I got cranky, he would just go into the bedroom and take a nap. I saw his retreats as being rude and uncaring. He saw my nagging as belligerent and critical. We were both right.

Then, when I recommitted my life to Christ, I began to realize that my behavior as Bud's wife was ungodly. All the things I had been doing and saying to him now looked and sounded ugly. When I started going to church, I noticed that the women I met in church didn't treat their husbands the way I was treating mine. Instead, they spoke gently to them. They looked at them with loving expressions. It seemed like they even *enjoyed* doing things for them. Watching their behavior told me that I needed to change. So I tried very hard to speak kindly to my husband. I wanted desperately to love him the way God loved me—unconditionally. I took my scepter of change and tossed it in the closet.

I also realized, however, that my husband and I were on

separate life paths. I was a Christian and he was not. I was forgiven of all my sins and he was not. I had a place in eternity,
and he was facing a Christless eternity. This just couldn't be.
My husband needed to be saved!

I charged back to the closet, found my scepter, and
launched into a not so subtle campaign to introduce my husband to Jesus. I left little Bible tracks around the house with
titles like *How to Become a Christian*. I turned on gospel music
five minutes before he came through the door. And every
now and then, when the occasion came up, I would let Bud
know that if he didn't give his heart to Jesus he would surely
go to hell, and I encouraged him to take care of the problem
soon. Armed with a righteous cause, I wielded my scepter
over Bud's head trying to force him to become something that
he really didn't want to be.

As my growth in Christ deepened, however, I began to
notice the wounds that my scepter was inflicting on him. Bud
felt intimidated by my unwanted sermons, he was jealous of
my newfound love for Christ, and felt separated from me
every time I shared how wonderful and exciting my relationship with Jesus was. My zeal for his salvation caused him pain
almost on a daily basis. I could see it in his eyes; I could feel
it in his touch. He no longer looked like the happy confident
man I married. Instead he had that look of a pound dog, the
one curled up in the corner of his cell because he's sure that
the people looking for a new pet will choose the cute little
attention-grabbing puppy in the cage next to him.

Then I heard a life-changing message during a seminar
on what it means to yield our lives to Christ. As the speaker
presented his points, I realized that I was trying to do God's
work for Him. I saw clearly for the first time that just as I had

done nothing to save myself, I could do nothing to save my husband. Just as I had been drawn to God through His unconditional love, my husband needed to be drawn to Christ in that same way. The pain of my regret led me to earnest repentance. With tears dripping from my face to my fingers, I lifted my heavy scepter of change up to my Master. I was finally free to love my husband without feeling the urgency to control him. My heart was free to be quiet and peaceful. Bud was free to discover what Christianity should look like: peaceful, joyful, kind, and gentle. More importantly, as I purposed to get out of Bud's face with the gospel, Jesus was able to come face to face with the man *He* loved and the one whom *He* was seeking.

When Bud left our home, I committed my time to praying for him as God's scepter was forging a path to where He and Bud could meet.

Though the pain of our separation was great, God tenderly led me one day at a time through the uncertainty I felt regarding our future. Our days without Bud were long and lonely, and our nights were even longer. I had no guarantee Bud would come back, and I could not promise my children that they would have their daddy home again. The only guarantee I had was that God would never leave us or give up on us and that He would continue to protect us and meet our needs. There was not one time during our separation when God failed to be our perfect heavenly Father. One month later, Bud returned and he had given his life to Christ.

According to the American College Dictionary a scepter is 1) A rod or wand borne in the hand as an emblem of regal or imperial power, 2) Royal or imperial power or authority; sovereignty.

Now a scepter can appear to be many things in the hands of a controlling woman. If it were a brush, I would have used it to repaint the Master's design for my husband and make him look like that dashing man in my teenage dreams. But today I think Bud is more handsome than any fictional character I might have manufactured on my own. His strength of character, his humor, his love for adventure, and his forgiving love for me is so appealing that a dark Italian on a white horse would pale in comparison to the man I have been blessed to spend my life being married to.

What does your scepter look like? A brush? A spatula? A knife? A needle? A pair of scissors? A computer? A calculator? No matter what form your scepter takes, your husband is not yours to paint, flip, cut, stitch, delete, or refigure. Though husbands and wives are to be joint heirs in the Master's kingdom, we are not joint owners. If our men need to change, nothing will do the job better than the scepter of righteousness held by the Master Himself.

When we stood at the altar, we got what we married, a man fashioned by the hands of our Creator, called to conform to His image through a renewed heart and mind. The Master will never ask us to give an account of how we changed our husbands, only of how we loved them.

Marriage Is Not a Heavenly Gold Card

Have you ever noticed how cleverly the pronoun *I* sits squarely in the center of the words *pride* and *sin*? Have you ever noticed how often you use the word *I* in your conversations? Do you ever find that your prayers have more *I*'s in them than you are willing to admit? The Impostor wouldn't have it any other way.

Credit cards are designed for *I* appeal. Gold cards are especially prestigious because they are given only to those credit card users who pay their bills on time. I like being one of the *special* credit card carriers. I know that I can get anything I want, anytime I want it. Of course when the bills come due, the glimmer of my gold cards lose their sparkle. So the best way I have found to keep them shiny is to not demand so much from them.

Marriage does not always purchase personal happiness or fulfillment. It does not necessarily secure our well-being. It can't guarantee financial stability, a fine home, or a closet full of clothes. It won't insure that our children will become respectable adults or go into full-time Christian service. It won't keep us from never feeling lonely, insecure, or frightened.

The day my husband came back to our home he was anxious to tell me about his amazing encounter with Christ and the angel who saved his life on the freeway. That day he was in his car headed in a very wrong direction. He was struggling with guilt for the things he had done and his part in bringing our marriage to a near end. Then, with the rain pelting on the pavement the little car he was driving hydroplaned across the freeway propelling him toward the center divider. Believing that he was about to die, Bud called out to God in a three-word prayer of salvation, *"I'm yours, God."* When his car came to a halt against the concrete barrier he opened his eyes and saw a silver Porche zigzagging across the lanes keeping the traffic from hitting him. As he watched the traffic moving slowly around him he realized that the man in the silver car had saved his life. When he turned around to wave his thanks, the car was gone.

For ten years we had been living in crisis management trying to survive from one fight to the next. Now, with my husband and I on the same life path, we were at last ready to reap the benefits of a normal marriage—or so I hoped. Normal, however, was not what I expected.

I thought *normal* meant that Bud and I would quickly become two spiritually mature people, raising two perfect Christian children, serving Christ side by side with peaceful happy smiles on our faces twenty-four hours a day. I thought we would wake up every morning and have devotions together and engage in deep conversations about spiritual things. I thought Bud would take me by the hand and say, "Honey, I'm the spiritual leader now. Let's start serving Christ together."

Instead, for the first several years after Bud became a Christian his spiritual growth was slow and unsteady. Bible studies and church were an uncomfortable fit for him. He didn't like to discuss biblical issues and he felt insecure praying out loud. Because I recommitted my life to Christ with such gusto I thought my approach to spiritual growth was the standard for what was *normal*. But Bud's profile as a new believer challenged my ideals.

Bud came to know the Lord in pieces. Trusting Christ with his life was a one-small-foot-in-front-of-the-other process. Whenever a particular piece of his life wasn't going well he would give that piece to the Lord. For about ten years after becoming a Christian, Bud held a lot of pieces in his strong masculine hands until the time came when he had only a few pieces of his life left to surrender. Now today his hands are wide open. He has a joyful growing walk with Christ.

Though I am very assertive in my quest for spiritual maturity, I can sometimes have more head knowledge than life application. I have times when my tongue still works before my brain has had a chance to censor my words. I still have times when I allow my enthusiasm for goals to fill my schedule with more things to do than is helpful for anyone. Bud and I still have very different personalities. And to my surprise, I have discovered that *normal* has nothing to do with how we grow as God's children. In fact the word *normal* is not a word used in Scripture to describe our spiritual growth or lack thereof. Maybe the reason it is not found in God's Word is because it is the Impostor's word for how we think things should be. If the Impostor can keep us focused on how we think things should be we will always be disgruntled with the way things are. Though the Master loves to watch His children grow, He gets no pleasure from spiritual forced labor camps.

The Impostor is wrong about marriage. When we identify what marriage is not, we defeat the Impostor's faulty claims and render him powerless to destroy the wonderful things that marriage is. A romance novel, a scepter, and a heavenly gold card are shallow substitutes for what the Master has designed for the union between a man and a woman.

WHAT MARRIAGE IS

The warm breath from my children's little noses pressing hard against the living room window kept me mindful of the mystery that comes from the changing seasons.

"Who brought the snow?"

"Look, pretty flowers."

"Rain, Rain, go away, please come back another day" (an Oregon favorite).

"Yea, the sun is out. It's time to play in the sprinkler now, Mommy!"

Each new season to a child seems like forever, but their mother knows how soon the snow will melt. They can wish together that summer would just come and stay, but it too will fade away when the leaves catch the blazing colors of fall.

Marriage also has its seasons. We may long for those perfect summer nights, but the Master knows that winter will come with all its fury and blow the warmth away. With our noses pressed against the glass, He is mindful of the seasons that are yet to come.

Marriage can either be a living, breathing entity of delightful moments or a cruel thief of joy. It has times of terrible boredom and times when hard work and diligent patience is the only thing that will keep it going until the next season comes. This is why the Master has invited us into His press box where we can see life through His eyes. In the throws of winter He reminds us, "See, I hold all your tears in My bottle. Nothing is ever wasted. I use the rain to grow the flowers, and the sun to make them bloom. My favorite times are when it has all withered away and the ground is covered in ice, because I know that spring is coming. The colder the winter, the more glorious spring will be."

We caught a glimpse of what marriage is not, now it is time to look at what marriage is.

Marriage Is a Love Story

The love story of our marriage did not begin when Bud and I met or when he asked me to marry him. It didn't even begin when we exchanged our wedding vows. Though our hearts were all aflutter when we declared our love for each other, the heartbeat of the Master was muffled somewhere in the background. It wasn't until the love of our flesh went into cardiac arrest that the sound of the Master's heart captured our attention.

I found the Master's heart for marriage the day I asked God to bring my husband home. Until that day I had been asking God to save my husband because our family needed him to be the finishing touch in our Christian home. I wanted Bud to become a Christian because I didn't want him to go to hell. And, I wanted Bud to become a Christian so that we could share the joy of knowing Christ together. I wanted Bud to become a Christian because I loved him. My reasons were all right and honorable, but they were incomplete because their sphere of concern was too small.

When word of our separation hit the neighborhood news line many of my neighbors to whom I had witnessed were left wondering just how powerful my God really was. Then the news hit the church I was attending and my dear friends were heartsick. Several members in our church body were dealing with heavy problems of their own. We were in a season of discouragement. As I saw how my situation was affecting the people around me, a new plea was added to my prayer and thus began a new understanding of the master's heart for marriage. My prayer went something like this:

Oh, God, I know how powerful You are. I know that You will never give me more than I can handle. I so need You to come and control this horrible mess that Bud and I have made of our marriage. But, Lord, so many people are watching us. Some need to know how real You are. Some need to know how sufficient

You are. My marriage has been laid in front of so many people, saved and unsaved and their faith needs to be encouraged. My children have heard me tell them about You, but now, God, they need to see beyond the words; they need to see You. Please come and show everyone: my children, my neighbors, my church family, and me that You are a powerful God who loves my husband. Show them that You love our marriage. Come and do whatever it takes to make Your name great in our home and in the presence of all these people. Delight Yourself by healing our home.

I meant every one of those words. I was no longer bargaining with God or begging Him to answer my prayers. I was surrendering my deepest heart's desire to Him. I realized for the first time that my marriage was about more than my family. It was about God's family. Marriage from the Master's perspective was about displaying His faithfulness to His people and to the world. This was my first real experience of coming into God's heart and meeting Him there.

That is when our love story began. God's heart for our marriage was now beating in my heart. Up to that point, I had not understood the way that God felt about marriage. I didn't realize how perfectly He has loved it since the beginning. His heart overflowed with joy the moment He saw the look on Adam's face when Adam woke up from his sleep and found Eve next to him. As He presented them before the audience of His creation, His plan for the world was in perfect working order. Walking with them in the Garden, listening to them talk to each other and with Him was what He had created them for. Through this sinless couple and through their offspring, all the world would be blessed for all generations. Before sin entered into the Garden, God's heart beat in perfect sync with the hearts of His first married couple.

When Bud came back home we were both in awe of the miracle God was doing in re-creating our marriage. To celebrate our new beginning, we decided to renew our wedding vows. Following the ceremony we went on a ten-day honeymoon to Hawaii. There, as we were lying on the warm sand drinking in the joy of being together, Bud reflected on what had gone wrong in our home. He said, "Sandy, all these years we have been playing at the game of marriage. I was husband and you were wife. I was Daddy and you were Mommy. But we were never friends." He was so very right. From that day on we worked at becoming friends with each other.

Though our friendship may have had rocky moments even after our reconciliation, we nonetheless always had our commitment to stay together forever to fall back on when our differences threatened to separate us all over again. Learning how to work in sync together has become a daily project as we follow God's heart for marriage.

A perfect example of this took place the day Bud's mother came to our home to die. We knew that we needed to work in perfect harmony with each other if we were going to be able to handle the heavy responsibilities that lay before us. Loving Mom was never an issue, but we each felt stretched beyond our comfort zone when it came to physically caring for all her bodily needs. So, the day before Mom was released from the hospital we prayed and committed together before God that everything that was before us to do we would do as a means of showing Mom how much God loved her. From that point on, we worked together like two hands in one glove. While I changed Mom's dressings, Bud helped her take her pills. While he helped her get her bed into a comfortable position I prepared her meals. We listened for her voice in the middle of the night and together we helped her to get to and from the bathroom. We were the hands of God created to do His good work as He prepared Mom's heart to come home to heaven.

Whether we have jobs that require both of us to work together or whether we have responsibilities that call us to work on our own, our hearts are learning to be so closely intertwined with each other, that they still beat as one. It's the greatest love story every written; God fashioned two hearts to beat as one with His.

Marriage Is a Mirror

When my daughter, Annette, got to the age where mirrors became the most important pieces of furniture in our home, we had a problem. We had only one bathroom mirror that we both could use while getting ready in the morning. Because the mirror was just big enough to fit the reflections of our two faces together, we learned to be very close while putting on our make-up.

Our times in front of the mirror provided great opportunities for sharing and laughing. We started out with faces that were only fit for each other to see, and we left with faces prepared for the world to see. This start to finish process removed any illusions we might have had about being naturally beautiful.

Marriage is a mirror that reflects who we really are—the good, the bad, and the glorious.

Throughout our marriage Bud has had plenty of time to study my moods. There is little I can do to fool him into thinking that I'm something I'm not. Sometimes that helps me to see who I really am, and other times it helps me to see where I need to change.

When my radio program was cancelled after five successful years, I went through a barrage of feelings. First, I had a great sense of confidence because I knew that God had allowed this to happen for a good reason. I was unclear as to what that reason might have been but I believed that when the door closed a window would soon be opened. However, after a few months of no paychecks and no clear direction for where I needed to be, I invited myself to a pity party for one. When Bud came home that night from work he found me curled up on the couch covered in a blanket and a blue mood. After a few attempts at trying to cheer me up, Bud finally got tough.

"Sandy, look at yourself. You're a beautiful, talented woman. Look at all the paintings you've done. I couldn't do that if my life depended on it. Look at all the things you've accomplished in your life. Look at all the friends you have and all the people you've encouraged. Look how important you are to me and to the kids. Why are you curled up in a ball acting as if your life is over? How much do you need to be happy?"

I couldn't find one single argument to fight back with. Even though I felt like a radio host *has been,* I was not ready for the glue factory. Bud told me the things he knew to be true about me. They were the good things about who I am. I am a woman created in God's image, called to do good works that He prepared for me to do long before I knew Him. I got up from my couch and got back into life because my husband reflected the right image back to me when I couldn't find my face in the mirror.

Yet, Bud's insight into my character can be just as reveal-ing in the negative areas of my life. One Saturday morning just winks after Bud and I woke up, I rolled over, tweaked his cheek, and said, "Okay, Honey, what are we going to do today?" To which he responded, "Well, we are going to do nothing today." Doing nothing in a day is about as close to death as I ever want to come. So I bit back, "Do nothing? We can't just do nothing. It's Saturday, there's lots to do. All we need is a good plan, and we can at least do SOMETHING!" Holding firmly to his position he stated his case one more time. "Sandy, all week I do plans. I'm tired of plans. Today I just want to sit and do whatever I feel like doing. Is that all right with you?" Then an idea flashed through my obsessive mind. "Oh, well here's what we'll do then. We'll just plan to not make plans. Then we can plan just the fun things we want to do." As Bud growled nasty things into his pillow, I saw an unflattering reflection of the ugly side of my charac-ter. I was controlling, compulsive, and condescending.

It's so much easier for me to receive from Bud the good things that he sees in me. It's when he reflects back to me the bad things, those things that continuously dog my flesh, that leaves me wishing he didn't know me quite so well. Yet, it is the full, unveiled insight into my character that helps me to see reflections of myself through his intimate understanding of who I am. God often uses the mirror of marriage to shape me and mold me to become more like Him.

But marriage is also a mirror that reflects what I believe to be true about who God is and what He is like. For instance,

God is omniscient, omnipotent, and omnipresent—He knows all things, He is all-powerful, and He is everywhere all the time. Though I know and believe this to be true, my marriage will often prove to me whether or not I *really* believe it.

God Is Omniscient

At the time that Bud left our home, I had friends who told me that I should file for divorce and accept that God was trying to rescue me from a life of being tied to a man who didn't love Him. A few went so far as to suggest that maybe God had a godly man waiting for me in the wings. God is omniscient. Therefore, I reasoned before God that if He knew everything that had happened in my life and everything that was going to happen, He alone knew what I needed to do to stay on course with Him.

At times when I wished for release from the pain of our marriage, God would whisper in my ear, *Not yet. Remember the father in the parable of the prodigal son? Sit on the hill with Me and watch for your husband's shadow coming around the bend. You see who he is today, but I see who he will be tomorrow. Wait with Me until tomorrow comes.*

Tomorrow has come. Today I can see the man God saw coming around the bend. Today I cannot imagine life without Bud. Kind, patient, thoughtful, friendly, fun, romantic, responsible, faithful, all that I had hoped for and more; he is the best part of my life. He was worth trusting the omniscience of God.

But what if Bud had not come home? What if our marriage had remained unchanged? Because of what I know to be true concerning God's all knowing character, I would still be able to lay all of my life before Him and trust Him.

Linda is a friend who endured treacherous abuse during her marriage. Though she tried to love her husband and to be a testimony of God's forgiving love to him, her husband only grew more temperamental and abusive. They were divorced. Did God fail her because the outcome of her circumstances were so different than mine? No. Was her life no longer a useful message to her family, neighborhood, and church? No. For just as God hates divorce because He loves marriage, He also hates violence. Linda's story of God's all-knowing love for her stands as a testimony of His protection and mercy. When the chosen daughters of the Master trust His omniscience they can rest in Him knowing that He sees the end of their lives from the beginning and can lead them through life's most difficult circumstances.

God Is Omnipotent

The more I learn to rely upon the power of God to change my husband the more I am free to be the loving wife that God has called me to be. Because I know that a home is best protected when husbands and wives pray together, I felt frustrated by the lack of ease Bud and I felt with each other in prayer. So, relying first on my flesh, I tried for a long time to force the issue. When arguments and tears didn't help, I would retreat and go back to relying on God to work in the hearts of both my husband and me. Then little by little, as serious situations that needed prayer came up, Bud and I would take each other's hands and bring our needs to God together. Tasting how wonderful it felt to pray with my husband would only increase my desire to pray with him more. But if I brought the subject up, Bud would bristle and I would go back to square one; trusting God to work in both of our hearts. Then out of the blue, Bud came upstairs one morning and said, "Honey, I know that you have been wanting for us to pray together for a very long time. I think we need to start doing that right now."

Whether or not I really believe that God is omnipotent is reflected through how I respond to the challenges that marriage presents me on a daily basis. Every time I try to manipulate our marriage through my own strength, I lose the joy of experiencing with God His omnipotent ability to fulfill His will in us through our union together.

God Is Omnipresent

Though a good theologian could define the omnipresence of God in deep biblical terms, I see the evidence of God's presence everywhere I turn. God's omnipresence is the present or the gift of His companionship.

Before my husband retired, his job required a lot of travel. I seldom worried about him when he went out of town. However, one day when he left for Panama, my heart was gripped with fear. "What if the plane went down in the ocean? What if the criminals who traffic drugs through the canal have a shoot-out and my husband gets caught in the crossfire? What if he just dies out there for no reason at all?" Fear doesn't need a lot of logic on which to base its arguments. I prayed for Bud, but I still felt an overwhelming sense of dread every time I thought of him in that far-off place. Then the mirror of marriage reflected the real problem. I didn't trust God with my husband's life. As I reflected back over all the times that God had protected him, I was reminded of what He has promised, "I will never leave you or forsake you." My panic turned to peace. I realized that God was not only present with me, He was present with my husband, and He was still present in our marriage. His presence is a present to both of us, every day, all the time, forever.

Marriage, by God's design, is a mirror that reflects the image of God in the church and through the church to the world. I believe this is the mystery that Paul referred to in Ephesians 5:31–32: "'For this reason a man will leave his father and mother and be united to his wife, and the two will become one flesh.' This is a profound mystery—but I am talking about Christ and the church." God, Jesus, and the Holy Spirit are three separate persons of the Godhead, distinct in their roles, yet identical in their essence and values. Their unique functions never conflict with their oneness. Because they are unmistakably the same in all they are, think, feel, and value, they are one in what they do. One can never disagree with, compete with, resent, or rebel against the other. They are one.

Marriage, according to God's heart, is to be a reflection of His oneness. His intention for marriage is to illustrate the oneness of the Trinity through the bond of holy matrimony. As individual marriages within the church reflect the unity of the Godhead, they bring the principles of the Trinity with them when they come together in the body of Christ. It is a mystery that can only be understood by understanding the Tri-unity of God.

Bringing husbands and wives into full oneness in Him is the ultimate purpose of the Master's heart for marriage. Couples who reflect Him in all they do are the backbone of the church. The church is the lighthouse that leads the world to Christ. Therefore, oneness in marriage is essential not only for the happiness of married couples but also for the kingdom plan of God.

It is the Impostor's goal to break the mirror of marriage, so he can stifle the growth of the Master's kingdom. He would love for us to always see life from his tarnished perspective, mirroring his love for independence and self-reliance and thereby leading us away from the intimacy that the Master's heart longs to have with us. Though we may not see everything God wants us to see yet, we can be sure that the more we shine our mirrors the clearer His image will be reflected in us, in our marriages, and through our churches.

MARRIAGE IS A GARDEN

Last year I planted alyssum. They were supposed to be delicate white flowers, and I intended them to line our driveway. However, within just a few weeks, my alyssum shriveled up into stringy brown patches of dead stuff. I decided rather than give up on them, to just water them as if they were still alive. The day came when little green leaves began to sprout from their lifeless stems. Soon there were tiny buds. Then the flowers started to bloom. To my surprise, they didn't resurrect as alyssum! Sprouting in their place was the most beautiful royal blue lobelia. How amazing!

When Bud and I were first married our marriage was very much like our little patch of alyssum. Our dreams for what we thought marriage should be dried up and fell to the ground one by one. Yet the Master did not give up on us. He continued to pursue us with His patient caring love and His desire to breathe new life into our hearts. Today our love stands strong and solid. It is a picture of what God does when He brings dead stuff to life.

I love a beautiful garden although I'm not a great gardener myself. The colors and the smells of flowers that are well cared for attract me to them. A well-groomed garden is a picture of life reminding me that the world was intended for life and beauty.

Last year I was invited to the home of Frank and Bunny Wilson to share in the celebration of their twenty-five years of marriage. Like Bud and I, Frank and Bunny have experienced the power of God breathing new life into their marriage. As a result, their marriage has become a brilliant reflection of God's heart.

While strolling through their back yard with another of Bunny's many friends, I made a comment about how beautiful their gardens were. She proceeded to explain to me that their yard had been a complete disaster. Dry grass, rocks, and weeds had all but taken over their yard. Then the Wilson's hired a gifted friend to transform their lot from an eye sore into a place where people could come to find peace and beauty. Today the lawn is green and lush. There are little walking paths that lead you from one lovely garden patch to another. It was totally inspiring.

Like Bunny, I have a brown thumb for plants. But I saw, through Bunny's garden, that maybe Bud and I could do something with the backyard that we had all but given up on. Our yard just sits there serving as a playpen for our dogs. There are no flowers—just a few trees and some grass. I shared my inspiration with Bud and for once we both have caught a glimpse of hope for our dreary yard. When spring comes Bud and I have decided to dig a few paths, plant a few flowerbeds, and we're even going to try to install a pond. I am looking forward to watching our yard be transformed into a place of beauty.

This is the plan for marriage from the Master's perspective. When we see what He can do in redeeming the love between two people we are inspired and encouraged to trust Him to do the same in us. Just as Bunny's yard spoke to me and motivated me to see what we could do with our pitiful piece of land, Bud and I want our marriage to be an example of what God can do when we hand our hearts over to Him.

When the Master breathes His life into a marriage, it will stand as a beacon of who He is. When husbands and wives reflect His character, they can't help but reproduce His character in each other and in others. People will see that God is wise, powerful, kind, forgiving, just, patient, gentle, longsuffering, joyful, peaceful, holy, and able to conquer any invader who would dare to destroy His Garden.

Now That We've Said, "I Do"

It was one of those rare days in Oregon when Bud and I had a chance to escape. We threw a few things together and pointed our car toward the beach. The ride became a game of "remember when's."

"Remember when we had breakfast at that little diner in Dundee?"

"Remember when you took the wrong fork in this road and we ended up lost in McMinneville?"

"Remember that funny lost dog we fell in love with in Newport, and the couple who said, 'His name is Rags and he belongs to you now'? Then we spent an hour trying to find another couple to give him to?"

Bud and I could look back over our lives together and count up all the difficult times we've had and remember all the hurtful things we've done to each other. Instead we chose to remember the good things the Master has done to restore the love we almost threw away because we didn't have His heart for marriage. Now with His heart beating in us we see that our marriage has a greater purpose than just our own happiness. Yet, when we allow God to write our love story, be our mirror, and grow us into an attractive garden, we find that we are more exceedingly happy together than we could ever have imagined.

The Impostor is horrified by the persistence of marriage. He would love nothing more than to destroy every marriage within God's kingdom. He knows the power that marriage has to derail his plans to bring down the Master's kingdom.

Two are better than one,
because they have a good return for their work:
If one falls down,
his friend can help him up.
But pity the man who falls
and has no one to help him up!
Also, if two lie down together, they will keep warm.
But how can one keep warm alone?
Though one may be overpowered,
two can defend themselves.
A cord of three strands is not quickly broken.

ECCLESIASTES 4: 9–12

The Call of the Imposter

Ah, so you want to know what marriage is! Marriage, my dear one, is anything you want or need it to be. You write the definition of marriage when you fall in love.

My call to you is this. Come away from the stress that has been imposed on you by those who believe there is some great eternal purpose in marriage beyond happiness.

No one, not the Master, not even I have the right to write the rules of marriage for you. It is a choice you must make. So if it feels good to you now, then enjoy it for now. If it becomes a burden, open your hands and let it go. I am here for you, to counsel you according to the truth that is within you. Follow my call and happiness will always be yours.

The Call of the Master

Listen to Me, my bride. Marriage is My creation. Marriage is My poem for you. You are a reflection of My character when you love each other the way that I love you. You are the portrait of the church when you build your marriage according to My heart. You are a testimony to the world of who I am.

I have a plan for your union that is more wonderful than anything you could have planned for on your own. Trust Me, I never change. I will never leave you to fend for yourselves. The two of you are better than one, and when I am in the center We are strong and powerful enough to weather any storm that might threaten to tear you apart. So stand against My enemy and come to Me. I will lead you through all the seasons of your marriage. This is the purpose I have designed you for. Now come with Me and see what I can do.

The Homeward Heart

Lord, you are my creator.
For you there is no poor, indifferent place.
Somewhere I have missed your will.
I am in a poor impoverished place where there is
little beauty of spirit, little music, color, or grace.
I want so much for my home to relfect you.
I want this to be a tiny taste of the eternal.
I would do anything to achieve it.
Please, Jesus.
Please come and make this a holy place.
Bring the Holy Home to my house.

CAROL BRAZO, *NO ORDINARY HOME*

CHAPTER FIVE

*S*tuck in a slow checkout line in the supermarket can give you all the time you need to catch up on the latest news and information. One afternoon there was a pricing problem going on with the person in front of me. The manager was called to verify the price of apples, and a stock person was running to get another gallon of milk for the customer while I stood wondering if my turn at the register would come before or after my next birthday. Then, as I perused through the myriad of magazines and tabloids, I noticed something very interesting as I read the titles of the articles in front of me.

"Preparing Your Home for the Holidays"
"Death House—The Menendez Murders"
"Lose Weight with Good Home Cooking"
"300-Pound Baby Born to 90-Pound Mother"
"Turn Your Shack into a Mansion with New Fashion Colors"
"Child Held Prisoner in Bedroom for 14 Years"

The extremes of what home might be like run the gamut from heavenly stories of shared love and acts of kindness to hellish tales of dark deeds that fill the soul with fear, anger, and resentment. For most, however, the word *home* conjures up pictures of families working hard to carve out lives that will be fruitful and rewarding. No matter where we fit on the scale, home is the place where our lives have their beginning. Every report we watch on the evening news began its story somewhere in the home. Yet, for all the influence that home has on each one of us, it is perhaps one of the most misunderstood establishments of our day.

Home is not a place where fashion is made famous. It is not a place where children are the celebrities in the family and parents become the bottomless checkbooks for their offspring. Home is not a motel for tourists who spend their days in search of exhilarating experiences and need a place to crash for the night. Home is not a retreat where parents hide their children from the evils of the world around them. Home is not a place where the big and strong lord their power over the weak and frail. Home is not to be found in the philosophies of the politically correct. And a sense of home doesn't just happen all by itself.

All homes need a maker to make them happen. Yet, in these times of unlimited opportunities, homemaking as a chosen career has become almost as irrelevant as elevator operators. Still, the position of homemaker is the only job I know that influences everything around us and leaves its mark on the world for generations to come.

The idea of home did not originate in the hearts of women. It began in the heart of our Creator who longs to give us His heart for the home. As with everything else that sin has corrupted, the Impostor has targeted our homes for destruction. But the Master will never allow His design for the home to be crushed by the treasonous acts of his enemy. Our homes are important to God; therefore, we as homemakers are important to Him also.

My heart for my home took on a whole new meaning when I first became aware, as a young homemaker, that my home was important to God.

I was cleaning the kitchen for the thousandth time that morning. Toys were strewn across the living room floor. There were piles of laundry waiting to be done and my ironing was dividing and multiplying in the back of the house. I was cranky and tired of being a slave to my family's socks and unmade beds. I didn't want to clean my house. I had cleaned it the day before, and it hadn't done any good; it just got dirty again. I began having that same old vision that had haunted me on other days. I started looking at what I *could* have been. I *could* have been a drama teacher like my drama teacher wanted me to be. I *might* have even become an actress or a singer or a famous artist. But no, I was a home-yukker. Nothing special, nothing fun, just cleaning up other people's messes for no good reason at all.

But something else happened that morning. I asked myself a simple question. *Sandy, if you were a teacher or an artist, would you really be happier than you are now?* Of course I said, "Yes, a million times yes!" But I knew the real answer was no. I had just begun my walk with Christ. My three-year-old daughter, Annette, had asked Jesus to come into her heart a few weeks before. She was proficient at memorizing Bible verses and sang the sweetest little Sunday school songs all day while she played. My husband hadn't yet given his life to the Lord, and I had another baby on the way. Suddenly it dawned on me. My home wasn't a waste of my time. My home *was* my career. It was my mission field. It was what I did for a living. It was what God had called me to do. I may not have known a lot about how to do it right, but at least I had an idea of what my purpose was.

Once I realized how much the Master loved my home, I began to see my home in a different way. I stopped thinking of myself as a housewife, someone who had married a small building with a yard. Instead I took the word *homemaker* and placed it after my name: Sandy Snavely—Homemaker. I liked the sound of it. I had the thought that Jesus loved the title as well—He is a homemaker also. He said: "'I go to prepare a place for you. And if I go and prepare a place for you, I will come again, and receive you unto myself; that where I am, there ye may be also'" (John 14:2b–3, KJV).

If Jesus doesn't feel that being a homemaker is a waste of *His* life, maybe we would do well to follow His example. He loves being our homemaker because He loves His home, and He went to great lengths to make us fit to live with Him there. Likewise, we cannot love being homemakers until we first love the homes we have been commissioned to make. I know firsthand how important it is to discover the Master's perspective and purpose for home. So I invite you to come with me and see the home as the Master sees it.

Home is a:

H—Harbor of Safety
O—Office of Character Production
M—Model for Wisdom
E—Expression of Heaven

HARBOR OF SAFETY

Although as a child I lived with abuse and alcoholism, no matter how difficult our lives were, there always seemed to be a home where I could go to feel safe when our home no longer was.

I swore that when I had a home of my own, it would be a place of safety for us. When I became a homemaker, I discovered that the fears families face can take different forms—perhaps not as large on the surface as the fears I faced growing up; but home, nonetheless, needed to be that harbor where we could face our fears, no matter what form they took, and find safety.

When our son, Dean, was about seven years old, he encountered his first battle with a bully. This stocky hulk of a kid raised his fist to Dean's nose and announced a new ten-cent toll for anyone who wanted to walk past his house. Dean came back home to borrow a dime. Though I wanted to impose a few things on the bully myself, it was obvious that my son didn't need an overprotective mommy to validate his sense of humiliation. Instead, we sat down together and reflected on God's promises to protect His children. We prayed for God to walk with Dean around the corner. Then Dean marched out the door to face the bully for a second time. He made it around the corner without a bruise.

Fears outside our homes can be just as frightening as the fears within. I realized that bullies come in many different forms. Criticism, peer pressure, unfair treatment, rejection, defeat, disloyalty, and more can threaten to undo us. Without the refuge of home to run to they just might win the battle. When we are tired, hungry, afraid, hurt, lonely, and defeated, home is the harbor where we should be able to come to find safety.

When my family comes through the door and shouts, "I'm home," they need to know that bullies will not be allowed to come in with them. For me, because I also have bullies that chase me home, this kind of safety means that when I am home I am safe.

Safe to be myself
Safe to fail
Safe to succeed
Safe to grow
Safe to speak my heart
Safe to love
Safe to laugh
Safe to cry
Safe to dream

One thing I ask of the LORD,
this is what I seek:
that I may dwell in the house of the LORD
all the days of my life,
to gaze upon the beauty of the LORD
and to seek him in his temple.
For in the day of trouble
he will keep me safe in his dwelling;
he will hide me in the shelter of his tabernacle
and set me high upon a rock.

PSALM 27: 4–5

OFFICE OF CHARACTER PRODUCTION

While I was growing up, I often thought of my big sister, Rosanne, as being a kind of goodie two shoes. She was also a bit of a wimp. Although she was three years older than I, I could easily knuckle her to the floor whenever she bugged me more than I could stand. One day Rosanne came home from school in tears. A classmate got mad at her during lunch and when Rosanne shot back with a pithy remark the girl slapped her. "What did you do?" I asked hanging on her every word.

"I just walked away with my head up high," she answered with a smug expression on her face.

I looked at her as if she were nuts. "Why didn't you just clobber her?"

Then Rosanne said something that I've never forgotten. "I would never consider stepping down to her level." That was the day my sister changed from a sissy to a lady.

I came from a family of fighters both verbal and physical. When my body ceased to grow as large as my temper, I just compensated through a venomous tongue. My tongue became my greatest asset and my enemy's biggest nightmare, but my parents were proud of the creative language skills that I had perfected. Their praise was all the encouragement I needed to keep up the good work of winning arguments with my words.

Once when my mother was on the phone with my aunt, I heard Mom yelling something into the receiver, and then she slammed the phone down and started to cry. I hated anyone who made my mother cry, so when my aunt called back I answered the phone.

"Sandy, your mother hurt my feelings and I am very angry with her."

The words rolled quickly off my eight-year-old tongue with the resonance of a southern belle, "Well la dee dah dah dah." Now most kids would have had their ear yanked off by then, but instead I turned and found Mom slapping her leg and laughing hysterically. This kind of praise didn't help me to learn to respect my elders.

Although my parents may have failed in some areas to teach me good character, they succeeded in others. My father was one of the most generous men I have ever known. He had a sympathetic heart for people in need and graciously gave away whatever he thought would be of use to someone else without a moment's hesitation or regret. My mother was a tough lady. No matter how often she felt beaten down by her circumstances she would inevitably come back fighting and she refused to let her circumstances keep her down. Instead, she got back up on her feet and started fighting to get back into life all over again. Dad's generosity and Mom's tenacity have helped me throughout my life to be a sharer and a survivor.

God has given us many words in the Scriptures that define how men of good character respond to life, and that outline the rewards good character brings. As the sin of our flesh seeks to pull us out of alignment with the holy character of God, His Word brings us back to where we need to be. Unfortunately, many of our biggest life lessons are learned through failure. Even our failures can become living testimonies of God's ability to reshape us according to His holy nature.

Home from the Master's perspective is a school where students learn how to make life work through the application of good character. From within the walls of home, God's promises and principles are tested and proven. Good character reveals how:

- Poverty can promote enterprise
  Star Parker grew up in poverty. She hated the stench of the projects but she felt defeated by the dis-

crimination she experienced due to her color. On and off welfare, Star eventually came to the realization that welfare was robbing her and her people of their self-respect and was sending her children the message that the government owes you a living. When she discovered God's storehouse of love and acceptance she decided to get off welfare and let God show her how to live according to His biblical principles.

Today Star has her own publishing company, printing materials that help others to develop productive lives. She is a national speaker. She is a tough-minded political activist. But more than the financial rewards, Star's children have a living example of God's sufficiency and His power to provide for the needs of His children when they give their needs to Him.

•Brokenness can bring healing

Sandra Simpson LeSourd was a bag lady in Billings, Montana. A group of godly women put Sandra's name on their top ten people that they wanted to see come to Jesus. Sandra's life hit the wall. She found herself in the mental ward of a state hospital. While she was there, Sandra met a woman whose fiancée had been killed shortly before their wedding. Though Karen was emotionally broken she nonetheless had not lost sight of God's goodness. One night when Sandra was in deep despair, Karen sat by her bed and shared the gospel of Jesus Christ with her. When Sandra gave her heart to Jesus her life made a dramatic change. Following several years of growth and healing, Sandra wrote a wonderful book called *The Not-So-Compulsive Woman.*

But the story didn't end there. While attending a workshop led by a popular speaker, Sandra was introduced to the man who had just given a very inspiring message. They quickly became friends and eventually fell in love. The bag lady became the wife of Leonard LeSourd, president of *Guideposts* magazine and the former husband of the late Catherine Marshall. Sandra's grown children have witnessed their mother's transformation and saw firsthand that when God changes a life, His changes are forever.

• Heartbreak can kindle forgiveness

Bonnie Floyd received a devastating call one day from the Caribbean. Her father and stepmother had been found murdered with two other people while they were on vacation. The killers were apprehended and stood trial for multiple homicide. While Bonnie sat in the courtroom her mind began to replay a conversation she'd had with her parents just a few months prior to their being killed. Before leaving their home, after having shared the gospel of Jesus Christ, she turned to them and said, "Promise me one thing; if you ever get in a position where you fear for your life that you will call on the name of Jesus." They promised her they would.

Then, while one of the gunmen, who had confessed to the crime, was giving his testimony, he made a stunning announcement. He told the court that the couple must have been Christians because he heard them praying before they died.

Bonnie's heart was overwhelmed with both rage and gratitude. She hated the man who sat there telling the sordid details of their death, but she was grateful that her parents kept their promise. It was then that God began to pour His compassion into Bonnie's heart for the man who stole her parents from her. Later Bonnie went to the prison and shared the gospel with him. The man who helped to kill her parents became a child of God. When the time of sentencing came, all but one, the one Bonnie interceded for, received the death penalty.

Today she still keeps in contact with her forgiven brother in Christ and looks forward to the day when she and her family will be reunited in heaven. Who knows how many people Bonnie's children will need to forgive as they grow up. But their mother's example of unconditional love will serve as a perfect pattern for them to follow.

• Failure can produce humility

By the time he turned thirty, John had achieved the most aggressive of his life goals. He became a general manager for a well-known company. Tall and proud he exercised his duties with an air of self-assured confidence. Successful at first, John worked nonstop—often at the expense of his family. But he was a man on the move. Several years into his job, however, things began to go sour. The success he enjoyed in the beginning was quickly slipping away. The profit margin had dropped and his employees resented his unattainable objectives. But John kept on going. Loyal to the bone, he thought his company would always back him up. But after a while the company also lost confidence in him. John resigned.

There is a new look of compassion in his eyes and an unmistakable kindness in his voice today. What happened to John? Humility happened, and it happened while he was still young enough for it to change his future. Today John has a thriving business of his own. But more importantly he is a living example to his family and friends of how God pours out His blessings on humble hearts.

• Temptation can harvest holiness

David loved beautiful women. One evening while he was in his bedroom looking out the window, he noticed a woman soaking in a hot tub on the roof. Lust ran through his veins. He wanted her more than his passions could stand. So he put on his most charming face and introduced himself to her. Though she was already married, they fell madly in love; but their seedy affair was to bring disastrous consequences. She became pregnant. David couldn't allow the news to ruin everything he had achieved, so he planned to have her husband killed. Everything should have been perfect except that David was driven to the brink of near insanity because of his guilt.

Then one day his friend confronted him exposing his knowledge of what David had done. David repented before God for his adulterous heart.

Though broken by the weight of his sin, he was restored by God's cleansing and forgiving love. A heavy price was paid for their act of adultery when their child died after it was born. A few years later, King David would look into his young son's face and tell him the story of the older brother who lost his life because of his father's failure to resist temptation.

Years after his father's death, King Solomon stood on the balcony of his immense palace looking at the women in his courtyard. He had acquired more wives and mistresses than any man could keep track of. Perhaps his father's story hung like a cloud over his heart as he penned these words, "Now all has been heard; here is the conclusion of the matter: Fear God and keep his commandments, for this is the whole duty of man" (Ecclesiastes 12:13).

• Rejection can grow perseverance

Dean was one of those energetic kinds of kids who people either loved to be around or avoided like a rash. There were many times when other parents would suggest that maybe Dean needed a lot more discipline to help him behave himself. Well, our son had all the discipline he could handle, but we knew that turning Dean into a calm child wouldn't happen while he was an adolescent. So, I coined an answer for those obliging parents that helped them and me to be patient with Dean while he was trying hard to grow up. My words went exactly like this: "Right now Dean's personality is just too big for his body to contain, but some day he'll grow into it." Dean often felt rejected by people who didn't understand his enthusiasm.

Since then, Dean has grown into his energy level, and he has become a patient, talented, and much appreciated music teacher in the state of Washington. Persevering through the tough times in his childhood has taught him the value of not giving up on himself. I know that Dean will be a great dad to his own energetic children when he becomes a father.

• Defeat can inspire hope

Gail wanted desperately to become a wife and mother. When she met the man she thought God had chosen for her, she looked forward with great joy toward their wedding day. Yet, as the day grew closer, Gail began to see things in her fiancée that troubled her. Finally, after much prayer, she called off the wedding. Her feelings of defeat were great, and she wondered if she would ever get married at all.

Several years later, Gail went to a friend's house for dinner while she was attending a conference in the city where they lived. There at the table she met her future husband. Gail was a nurse whose specialty was in caring for cancer patients. He was a widow whose young wife had died of cancer. She always wanted to have a daughter named after her mother Diane. His daughter's name was Diane. She loved Jesus. So did he. They were married soon after they met. Gail and her husband have become a living witness to their children of how hope washes away the pain of defeat.

We have been instructed by God to apply ourselves as parents to teaching our children how to live holy lives by walking through life with them and by showing them what good character looks like through our words and through the successes and failures in our own lives.

These commandments that I give you today are to be upon your hearts. Impress them on your children. Talk about them when you sit at home and when you walk along the road, when you lie down and when you get up. Tie them as symbols on your hands and bind them on your foreheads. Write them on the doorframes of your houses and on your gates. (Deuteronomy 6:6–9)

I believe these words encourage us to do more than go on nature hikes with our kids, teaching them the difference between Creationism and Darwinism. I think they are reminders to us that we must take every lesson we have learned and are learning in life, put it in perspective with God's Word, and share what we have learned with our children. As homemakers we have been given the awesome opportunity to daily teach our children that God's promises and principles are the only sure foundation upon which we can build our lives.

The things we teach our children will follow them throughout their lives. They are useful to them no matter how old we are when we learn them or how grown they are when we put them into practice. It is never too late to start showing your children that good character is important to God. It is the evidence of God's character working in us and in our homes. It proves to our families and to the world that God's ways work.

MODEL FOR WISDOM

The wise woman builds her house,
but with her own hands the foolish one tears hers down.

PROVERBS 14:1

If I could go backward in time there are many things I would have done differently and much that I would have done better.

I would have encouraged my children to slow down more and to hurry up less. I would have nitpicked less and encouraged more. I would have said yes more often than I said no. I would have endured their messes while they were learning to create the things that were brewing in their imaginations. I would have lectured less and listened more. I would have told them more about my failures than I did about my successes.

When, however, we wallow in the things we didn't do or should have done, the Master is mindful of the other side of the story. He remembers every good that we have done in His name. He remembers the kindness we have shown our family and others. The lessons we learned from our failures and our willingness to teach them to our family have not been lost in His memory. He treasures the godliness that we have allowed Him to build into our lives. He is quick to recall the forgiveness we continue to shower upon our family's mistakes. He fondly acknowledges the hope we hold out for our children as they go off on their own.

When we need encouragement as homemakers we can go to Him and ask Him if there might be anything in His record book that will help us to remember the good work He has done through us. These bits of comfort, however few or many, are like markers that help us to see that we are on the right track. They inspire us to keep going when we feel like nothing we've done has been of value.

Perhaps these backward glances of the Master are the reason why Paul gave these words to the women in Crete:

> Likewise, teach the older women to be reverent in the way they live, not to be slanderers or addicted to much wine, but to teach what is good. Then they can train the younger women to love their husbands and children, to be self-controlled and pure, to be busy at home, to be kind, and to be subject to their husbands, so that no one will malign the word of God. (Titus 2:3–5)

Some of the saddest women I have ever seen are the ones who refused when they were young to take their role as homemaker seriously. Many of them can be found sitting alone in their homes feeling angry and bitter for the way their families have deserted them. Others sit on bar stools drinking away their guilt. But in between the extremes are the women who have allowed the Master to teach them how to be good moms, loving wives, and lovers of their homes. They have become a living resource for all the younger women around them who have just begun their journey through homemaking. Having been wisdom-gatherers along the way, their lives shine as worthy models of how wisdom builds a home.

If we could combine everything that they have learned and put it into a poem wouldn't it be a wonderful symbol of what we want to be like as we grow into our role as a home-maker? We have been given such a poem. It's called the Proverbial Woman. She is God's model described for us in the Book of Proverbs, chapter 31. She is a composite of the many women who have cherished their role as homemakers. But beware, it's a long poem. One quick read through and you may feel like there aren't enough vitamins in the world to give you that much energy. However, as the old joke goes, the only way to eat an elephant is to eat him one bite at a time. In this case, the only way we can become a reflection of this godly woman is to examine what she is like and ask ourselves one question at a time:

What would it take for us to—

- Be a trustworthy wife? (v. 11)
- Do good to our husband instead of evil and uphold his reputation in our thoughts, words, and deeds? (v. 12)
- Work in our homes with a good attitude, using what we have been given to meet our family's needs? (v. 13)
- Feed our family well-balanced healthy meals? (v. 14)
- Get up before the rest of our family and be ready to help them start their day with a smile? (v. 15)
- Take good care of our appliances? (v. 15)
- Be resourceful with our finances? (v. 16)
- Take care of our own bodies so that we will be physi-cally fit? (v. 17)
- Enjoy the results of our labor? (v. 18)
- Be near to our children to comfort them when they cry out in the night? (v. 18)
- Care for the needs of others in our neighborhoods, communities, and churches? (v. 20)

- Make sure our families have coats in the winter and shorts in the summer? (v. 21)
- Dress appropriately for all occasions? (v. 22–23)
- Behave in a dignified manner? (v. 25)
- Be optimistic about the future, knowing our God is sovereign over all things? (v. 25)
- Teach our children with kindness, love, and patience? (v. 26)
- Not spend our time watching soap operas, but maintain an efficient household? (v. 27)
- Do all that is on our plates with a servant's heart as we show our family what God looks like and how wonderful heaven will one day be? (v. 30–31)

No matter how you cut it, the job of being a homemaker is tough. But the Proverbial Woman is the woman who wisely builds her house knowing that she is empowered by God to do what He has called her to do. Therefore, His omniscience (His all-knowing, all-wise nature) already knows what we need before we even begin to tackle the job. His omnipresence (His all-powerful nature) already dwells within us to give us the strength to get started and to keep going. His omnipresence (His all-present nature) will not leave us without His presence to guide us through each day.

God is the God of "yes we can." The Impostor wants us to feel exhausted by the work that remains to be done in making our homes. Therefore, he will do all he can to keep us from accepting the proverbial challenge. But the Master is wise to his enemy's ways and His wisdom is the wisdom through which He will lead us to victory.

So go ahead, love your home, spit polish it, care for it, nurture it, be joyful in it, and treasure it for all it's worth.

EXPRESSION OF HEAVEN

Did you ever wonder as a child what heaven was like? When a loved one died and others said, "Oh, they have gone home to heaven," did you find their words to be a comfort or a curse?

While I was on my way to Alabama after the news that my mother had suffered a serious stroke, my mind whirled with memories of my mom and the life she had lived. The word *home* was perhaps one of the most painful words in her vocabulary. She grew up in Chicago where the Italian side of her family was at constant odds with the Greek side of her family. Though divorce was unheard of in her day, her parents couldn't survive their cultural differences and her family became the only family she knew who was divorced. Though her father had a good income, he nonetheless refused to adequately support the family he left behind. With deep bitterness my mother remembered her two-year-old brother dying of diphtheria in her mother's arms because they couldn't afford a doctor's care. Her mother often wounded my mother's heart with words of criticism and rejection. One day while Mom was sitting in her mother's lap, her mother looked down at her and said, "Tootsie, I love you very much but I love your sister Marie more." No wonder *home* was not a word that felt good to my mother.

While on the plane, I asked God to not let my mother die until I knew if she knew Him. When I finished praying I felt God press these words upon my heart. "Sandy, not only does she know Me but I know her."

How comforting were those words to me. Though others may have seen some of my mother's ways to be a bit wild and unpolished, I knew my mother. I knew how hard her life had been, and I knew how her strong will to survive kept her going long after many would have thrown in the towel. Because I knew my mother so well, I was able to have compassion for her when her behavior would press me to the end of my patience. But God also knew my mother. He knew her fun spirit and her vulnerable heart. He knew her strengths and her weaknesses and He knew the simplicity of her prayers. God knew my mom.

Then God deepened His words to me. "Sandy, I am sending you to Alabama to help your mother die." My mother made no secret of the fact that she was terrified of death. Now, with my mother's life hanging in the balance, I struggled to know how to help her look forward to going home when home had always been a place of condemnation and unhappiness.

Later, as I stood next to my mother listening to her struggle for breath, the nurse informed me that Mom's brain had suffered so much damage that she was no longer responsive to touch or sound. Nevertheless I held her hand and said, "Mom, it's Sandy. I'm here. I love you." As I repeated those words over and over again, Mom suddenly squeezed my hand.

I continued talking to her and as I stroked my mother's forehead words began to flow easily from my lips. "Mom, it's all right for you to go home now. Jesus is waiting for you, and He loves you so very much. Mom, heaven is the most wonderful place you can imagine. There is love and joy everywhere. There are colors in heaven that you have never seen before. I'll bet you're going to be able to paint in heaven, and I want you to paint a picture of Jesus and have it waiting for me when I get there. Mom, you don't have to be afraid. God loves you and He knows that you love Him. Thank you for all the things you did for me. I will always love you." Then my mother pulled my hand up close to her chest and held it tightly while tears fell on her cheeks.

The next day my mother went home.

HEAVEN'S PATTERN FOR HOME

Home is an earthly expression of a divine concept. Or at least that is the way it is intended to be. But the Impostor also has a plan for home. Because everything the Impostor loves has independence woven into it, his plan for home follows particular patterns where independence is a part. Once we know the Master's heart for home, the imitations are easier to spot.

When women get together we talk, and as we talk we reveal through our words what we believe about home. Phrases like, "I just can't stand when things are out of order," "I am a clutter bug and my family just has to learn to deal with it," "I never cook, it's just not my thing," or "When I diet, everybody diets with me" reveal the independence that guides many of our homes. It is this spirit that the Impostor loves to hear because that is the kind of homemaker he is. Yet, phrases like, "My family enjoys being able to find what they need in their closets," "My family loves to sit around the table for a home-cooked meal," "I want my home to be beautiful but comfortable for everyone to enjoy," and "I love being a homemaker," sicken the soul of the Impostor.

While the Impostor's approach to homemaking centers around independence, the Master's heart for home centers on service. Jesus said, "I go to prepare a place for you." In preparing our place, He is serving us so that when we go to live in His home we will be able to reap the full joy of what His home is like.

In heaven the Master is the object of all affection. His home is inhabited with praise. His home is well ordered and perfectly kept. His home is holy. His home is radiant in glory. His home is equipped to meet the needs of all its inhabitants. His home is filled with meaning and purpose. There is great joy in His home. Worship of the Master flows freely. Love permeates everything. His home is the hope of the human heart when death threatens to steal life away; it is a refuge providing safety from all that's evil.

The Master's home is perfect because He is perfect. Though we have not been given all the details of what heaven is like, we know that however God commands us to be on earth is how we will be in heaven. Therefore, all the sin that plagues us on earth will be forever absent in heaven.

Our role as homemakers is to bring our home into alignment with our heavenly home. To do this we will need to love our earthly homes the way God loves our heavenly home. And we will need to know how to pray the way that Jesus instructed us. "After this manner therefore pray ye: Our Father which art in heaven, Hallowed be thy name. Thy kingdom come. Thy will be done in earth, as it is in heaven" (Matthew 6:9–10, KJV).

God's chosen people of Israel had a hard time being an expression of God's heavenly home. When God spoke to Moses on Mount Sinai, He unveiled to him what He Himself is like and how His kingdom is ordered. Moses then delivered those heavenly principles to the people who were living lawlessly in the valley below. God gave the laws to His earthly people through Moses so they would know how to restrain sin and how to govern themselves according to the holiness of heaven. The Ten Commandments became the house rules for the household of God.

Our households cannot survive without a clear set of house rules. From heaven to Moses to us, these commandments still express what heaven is like and how our homes should be modeled.

From God	To Moses (Exodus 20:1–17)	To Us
1. In My home, I alone reign in glory and majesty. No other god can sit in My place.	1. I am the LORD your God….You shall have no other gods before me. (v. 2–3)	1. In our home, God will be honored and obeyed.
2. In My home, I alone am worshiped and praised.	2. You shall not make for yourself an idol in the form of anything in heaven above or on the earth beneath or in the waters below. (v. 4)	2. In our home, God is the One true God and we will worship no other gods but Him; nothing we can earn or build with our hands or conceive in our minds or yield our passions to will be worshiped in His place.

From God	To Moses (Exodus 20:1–17)	To Us
3. In My home, My name is always honored and praised.	3. You shall not misuse the name of the LORD your God. (v. 7)	3. In our home, God's name will be held in the highest esteem in all we say and do.
4. In My home, every day in heaven is a holy day.	4. Remember the Sabbath day by keeping it holy. (v. 8)	4. In our home, the Sabbath day will be faithfully celebrated in God's house with His people.
5. In My home, all of the inhabitants are part of My family and they all honor Me.	5. Honor your father and your mother. (v. 12)	5. In our home, parents will be respected and honored.
6. In My home, death is nonexistent.	6. You shall not murder. (v. 13)	6. In our home, life born and unborn will be treasured.
7. In My home, everyone is faithful in their love to Me.	7. You shall not commit adultery. (v. 14)	7. In our home, marriage will be honored, and we will all live in purity and faithfulness.

From God	To Moses (Exodus 20:1–17)	To Us
8. In My home, I supply everyone's needs to the fullest degree.	8. You shall not steal. (v. 15)	8. In our home, honesty will govern over everything we do, and we will trust God to meet all of our needs.
9. In My home, My Truth resides everywhere.	9. You shall not give false testimony against your neighbor. (v. 16)	9. In our home, the reputations of all people will be highly regarded.
10. In My home, everyone is satisfied with all that they have been given from Me.	10. You shall not covet. (v. 17)	10. In our home, envy and jealousy will not rule over us.

HOME TO THE FATHER'S HEART

"I'm going home!" These three words might be the most important words ever spoken. In any language, at any age, they declare a return to the place where we belong. They are the words that remind us that somewhere there is a place where we are loved, known, and accepted. When we cross the threshold of home, we will be safe. The people who share our name will be there—waiting for us to come through the door.

Though the joy of these three words may have lost their

significance for some whose earthly homes have left their hearts in ruins, they remain nonetheless a hope for a better home yet to come.

Every home needs a maker. If you have felt that being a homemaker is a thankless job requiring too much of your time to do menial tasks that drain you of your significance, let me encourage you to come home to the heart of the Master. He loves your home. He wants to love your home through you. He longs to help you make your home a reflection of what is to come.

Being a homemaker is the job that the Impostor doesn't want us to take seriously. He wants us to flounder in it, run from it, or trivialize its importance. He fears how success will influence our families, our churches, and the world around us. Therefore, we must fight all the harder to resist his attempts to add our homes to his pile of rubble.

Can you imagine what will happen if we, as God's home-makers, follow His design for the home? Our homes will become a place where safety, good character, and wisdom flourish and where the expression of heaven causes others to look forward to their eternal home where no one will ever have to leave it or say good-bye again.

But just think of stepping on shore
And finding it heaven
Of touching a hand and finding it God's
Of breathing new air and finding it celestial
Of waking up in glory
And finding it home.

FROM THE SONG "HOME," AUTHOR UNKNOWN

The Call of the Imposter

Home is the place where people can grow up. Isn't it time you did just that? You are too valuable to tie yourself down to a place that is far too unmanageable for you to handle. Don't let your expectations for what you think home should be rise above what you can do.

Home is not a place where little puppets move according to some great Master plan. Do those houseguests of yours need you to be a great example to them of how to live? Absolutely! So do it—live! But, live the way I have shown you by being self-expressive and carefree. This is the goal of home—where people in the house honor the qualities that belong only to them. Don't be so codependent that you think they will die if you cannot become the queen of Homemakersville. Such drivel will enslave you to a life of antiquity.

Let your home glorify freedom and independence—in this you will be praised and honored.

The Call of the Master

I have prepared a place for you that is more wonderful than your mortal mind can imagine. It is alive with beauty and it is filled with praise. All of its residents dwell together in perfect peace and harmony. There is no sin in My habitation, and nothing within My gates suffers the corruption of the Impostor's lies. It is My home and it is waiting for you.

I desire for all things on earth to be done as they are done in heaven. Let your home be a refuge and a place where everyone who comes inside will find safety, peace, and unconditional love. I want your home to be a lighthouse that will guide others to Me who have no hope for rescue.

The principles in My home will teach your family how to live and how to endure life's trials and temptations. Honor these principles and you will be victorious. Take care of your home. Make it a place that is fit to be My dwelling. Make it a hint of what is to come when eternity opens its gates to you.

A New Heart
for Mom

I have no greater joy
than to hear that my children
are walking in the truth.

3 JOHN 4

anted—woman to fulfill the role of mother for children in need of constant attention. She must be able to cook, clean, transport young athletes to and from practices, and be their cheerleader in all sporting events. Previous experience is not required. The person who fills this position must be flexible, willing to give up her own identity and to set aside all previous aspirations of her own. Her sole purpose in life for the next twenty years will be to cater to the whims of her children while at the same time preparing them to be responsible, well-mannered adults. Upon hire, she will answer to, "Mom, Mommy, Mother, Ma," or, "Hey, You," and cheerfully execute her duties without executing her subjects. On the job training in nursing, counseling, and tutoring is a must. Though the starting pay is minimal, benefits and rewards may be a plus depending on the children's productivity—to be determined at a time after they have grown up, graduated from college, gotten married, and become parents. This job is not for wimps—women seeking glamour need not apply.

Perhaps one of the greatest lies fed to women by the Impostor is contained in the above job description. Causing women to believe that motherhood is cruel and unusual punishment for having ovaries has succeeded in bringing him closer to his goal of destroying the kingdom of the Master.

The Impostor's strategy has always been to draw the hearts of God's children away from the heart of the Master by turning their focus on themselves. Because of the incredible bond that is built between a mother and her child, drawing a mother's heart away from her child and onto herself has never been an easy task. In these times, however, he saw a few women who were ripe for the picking. He could feel the pulse of their passions as they yearned to break free from the enslavement of their roles as women. He knew their hearts would be easy to capture so with his plan in hand he headed in their direction.

Upon his arrival he gathered them around him and bound them together with a common cause. Then he helped them to formulate the basis for their cause by using children as the symbol of their oppression. Feeding upon their independent spirits he used their voices to spread *his* message to the world.

- Women must make personal fulfillment their highest priority in life.
- Women have the right to choose when and when not to have a child.
- Women are not only equal to but superior to men.
- Women can have it all.

There it was. The successful transmission of this message would accomplish his desire to destroy the family by turning the mother's heart away from her children and toward herself.

Just decades ago, many of us laughed when a band of bra-burning feminists first spewed their propaganda to the world. Yet as time wore on, their message seemed less bizarre. As if hypnotized by the gurus of the age, many of the women who scoffed at the "do your own thing" rhetoric of the 70s raised their daughters "to do their own thing" in the 80s. Today the message has changed again. Our love for home and children is on its way back. Some believe this resurgence of love for family is an indication that the Impostor is losing the battle for the mother's heart. But what if this is just another of his tactics to keep women centered upon themselves in a new way?

I recently read a popular book written by a woman who discovered that home was the better place to be. After building a successful career with lots of power and glamour, she had children. Soon the adorable ways of her babies won their way into her heart, and she left her career behind to stay at home. As I first began to read her story of how she surrendered her life to motherhood, I was warmly encouraged. However, by the end of the book, I realized that although she was now home enjoying her family, she was nonetheless still under the spell of the Impostor's ideals. Though she was part of the new wave of women today who are returning to their roots, her reasons for coming home to motherhood still had the aura of independence.

Those who follow trends seem to agree that women today are running back home by the droves after finding that careers are a poor substitute for being there when their children take their first steps. Yet their reasons are just as often motivated by independence as their reasons for abandoning motherhood were just a few years ago. Still having part of the Impostor's mindset, many women today believe that motherhood is all about them. Children have become just another way of making them feel better about who they are as women. Like for the woman in the book I read, motherhood has provided a better kind of high than having a career. Yet exchanging one high for another is not a sign of improved health. It is, however, a sign that the Impostor is still at work in mothers' hearts.

Our leanings toward independence will not be set straight until we allow our hearts to come into alignment with the heart of the Master and discover His heart for motherhood.

IN SEARCH OF A MOTHER'S HEART

Before the birth of our first child, my independent spirit kept me on the path of self-fulfillment. I was unhappy, and I was constantly looking for something or someone who could fill the empty places in my heart. School, taking leading parts in plays, the accumulation of friends, and even marriage hadn't yet satisfied my cravings for fulfillment. Motherhood was yet another step toward finding the missing something that I was searching for.

At first, motherhood made me feel that at last I had found my niche. As Annette's little heart began to beat within me, my life made a dramatic, though short-lived, course correction. I experienced a profound sense of wonder when my daughter was born. I looked at her wrapped tightly in her receiving blanket, and I realized that I had become a life-giver. I held a new person in my arms. She was more than just my child—she was a whole separate human being who depended on me to continue to give life to her. Her present and her future were snuggled against me, and I was terrified.

So I began my journey into motherhood searching for a formula that would guarantee ideal results. For years I worked my fingers to the bone trying to be the image of the perfect mom as portrayed on TV. Having grown up under the influence of the *Donna Reed Show,* I put on my shirtwaist dress and a string of pearls and did my best to become the ultimate mother. I baked, I cooked, I cleaned, and I erected all sorts of homemaking idols that I expected my whole family to worship with me. They didn't. What they often saw instead was only the intensity of my desire for fulfillment.

While on my way to ruining my children's lives through my drive to find happiness via mothering, I came upon a new way of understanding my heart—I found God's heart through the story of creation.

Although I had read the story a hundred times before, something new jumped out at me from the pages of my Bible. As I began reading the first chapter of Genesis, my attention was drawn to how often God looked at His work and said, "It is good." It appeared to me at first glance that God might have had an ego problem. He applauded His own work with unabashed pleasure each time He made something new. But because I know that God is holy, I knew He couldn't also be conceited. Upon further reflection, I realized that God was defining for me through His affirmations "it is good," what *good* really was. This put a whole new spin on how I looked at my work at home with my children. If everything that God does is good, then the things I do for His sake and according to His ways must also be good. When my work is all about Him instead of all about me, I can look at it and see that it is "very good."

While some may say that it is important for us to validate

our own work with self-affirming praise, I discovered that I needed instead to validate God's work by acknowledging His good works being fulfilled in and through me. "It is good" became a regular part of my conversation with God. When I showed His patience toward my children I would say, "It is good." When I sacrificed my own needs to meet their needs, I would say, "It is good." When I got up in the middle of the night to comfort them after a nightmare or give them cough syrup or clean up their intestinal eruptions, I would say, "It is good." Eventually, I began to realize that my heart for mothering was changing. I saw that what I did as a mother mattered to God. His stamp of approval began to mean more to me than filling up my happiness cup. Whenever I attached "it is good" to what I did, I exalted God for His creation of me as a mother. "It is good."

Good mothering begins in the heart. It is the result of allowing the qualities of the Father's heart to become the essential qualities of our own hearts. As I have sought to know my Father's heart, I have found six essential qualities that have helped me to know how to follow the pattern He has set in front of me. I believe these are vital for any woman who finds herself in need of a new or improved mother's heart. They are the qualities about which we can say when we put them into practice, "It is good."

1. A SAVED HEART

One day while Annette and I were puttering around in the kitchen I said to her, "Annette, do you remember when you asked Jesus to come into your heart? You were only three years old but you understood that Jesus died for your sins, and you really wanted Him to be your Savior. I haven't talked to Dean about Jesus yet, and he's already four years old."

Annette responded to my concerns with, "Oh, I just told him about Jesus the other day, and we knelt by my bed and he asked Jesus to come into his heart. So, it's okay, Mommy, I already took care of it."

How amazing—Annette led Dean to Jesus, and it was so natural to her that she didn't even think to share the experience with her mother. Yet she understood how essential it was for her brother to have Jesus in his heart. So without any reservations or fears of forcing a decision before he was ready, she became an evangelist to a four-year-old.

If the only way we can come to the Father's heart is through Jesus, then the same holds true for our children. The problem some of us have is in acknowledging that our children are sinful and need a Savior.

A couple of years ago a string of robberies were committed in the Portland area by a gang of teenagers. The pattern for the thefts showed that with each robbery, they became more and more brazen. After several successful jobs were done, the police closed in on the culprits. The ringleader of the group was the son of a well-known Portland attorney. Somehow the kid was able to slip out of the country before he was arrested. Word got back to the authorities that he was living in luxury in Mexico paid for by his parents who were trying to protect their child from having to do what other criminals do—go to jail. When we try to be our children's saviors we prove our arrogance toward God.

The heart is deceitful above all things and beyond cure. Who can understand it? (Jeremiah 17:9)

It is no secret to God that we are sinful and deceitful from birth and that we have no hope for recovery apart from Him. If we want to know the Father's heart for motherhood, we will have to deal with the issue of sin in our children's lives. It is not always easy to accept that our children are just as sinful as the neighbor kids down the street. Though our hearts may melt at their lovable ways, we cannot ignore that the day will come when their flesh will begin to show itself through intentional, purposeful, and rebellious acts. They will lie, cheat, steal, and behave in ways that you never thought they would when they were tiny cherubs sleeping sweetly in their cribs. Sin is not just a phase. They will not grow out of it. We cannot buy it off, dress it up, or will it away. God cares about our children's salvation.

God is not shocked by our children's need for Him. Jesus loved children. When He saw them running around playing and pestering their way through the crowds coming to hear Him speak, Jesus opened His arms to them and gave them a bear hug from heaven. His gentle love enveloped them, and I doubt that even the youngest one there ever forgot the touch of Jesus' hand. When they grew up, I'll bet they couldn't wait until their own children were able to sit still long enough to hear the story of the day their mommy met the Savior. When the story was finished, I wonder if they heard a voice whispering in the background, "It is good."

2. A SANCTIFIED HEART

Whether you turn to the right or to the left, your ears will hear a voice behind you, saying, "This is the way; walk in it." (Isaiah 30:21)

Everyone in my family is a good cook. For years I watched my mother grab handfuls of ingredients, put them in a pan, and when it came out of the oven, it was heaven in a dish. My sister, Rosanne, has a microchip in her brain where recipes are stored. She seldom refers to a book when whipping up biscuits, breads, or cakes. Even my brother, Kenny, has a knack for knowing how to throw something wonderful together in a moment's time. Rubbing shoulders on a daily basis with these natural epicureans somehow gave me the idea that I could experiment with food without first learning how to follow a recipe.

Years after the fact, my family still finds opportunities to tell the story of fish soup. While doing an imitation of my mother in the kitchen, I decided to make a new kind of meal with fish. A few tomatoes, some spices, water, and whatever else I could find hiding in the refrigerator, and dinner would be on the table—fish soup—pieces of opaque fish floating on top of some reddish gruel. Unfortunately, it tasted worse than it sounds. Of all the great meals I have served my family, the only meal they seem to remember is the one that should have never been.

I thought because I grew up with good cooks all around me that cooking was imbedded in our family genes. Instead of studying what flavors blended well with others and instead of learning how to measure accurately, I spent years indiscriminately experimenting with food. The results of my haphazard approach to feeding my family can be summed up in two words: fish soup.

God wants more for our lives than fish soup. Our hearts have been chosen and reserved for righteousness. Therefore, we need to learn how to love what the Master loves and how to hate what the Impostor loves. This takes time and training, and it is motivated by a deep love for the Master and a desire to become more like Him. This process of growth is what sanctification is. Sanctification is the process of changing our sin habits into acts of godly behavior. Families share many things, from our gene pool to our sin pool. How sin is acted out in our lives is very likely to be passed on to us through our environment, especially through our homes.

We all have a bent toward certain sins. Yours are different than mine, but you have them nonetheless. Without the ongoing work of sanctification, our children will not only mirror our sin habits, but they will creatively add a few of their own to the list and in time will become even better at sin than we were when we were their age. Sanctification is learning how to straighten out these "bents" by learning how to live a Christlike life.

How we grow in our walk with Christ will have a trickle down effect on the lives of our children. Just as a mother who has a tender love for Jesus can inspire her children to follow her example, the opposite is also true. A mother who applies herself to her spiritual growth with as much energy as she gives to memorizing her shopping list in Hebrew might have a hard time convincing her children that they need to live like Jesus lived. We cannot teach what we do not know.

Many of us struggle against busy schedules to find time to be consistent in how we teach our children. It is important for us to teach them to pray, read the Bible, and to develop good, healthy friendships with their friends at church. What we fail to realize, however, is that our lack of spiritual training teaches a lot to our little ones. We teach them that God is not really interested in their daily lives. And we teach them that there is nowhere for them to turn when they are faced with the temptations of the world, the flesh, and the Impostor.

We and our children have three forces working against us to keep us from learning how to live the Christian life. These three forces cover every area of our lives. The flesh, the world, and the Impostor work together to keep us away from the heart of the Master.

Forces Within (The Flesh)

On the night before Christmas, many years ago, I went upstairs to say good night to our children. They had been so full of holiday excitement that it seemed to take forever to get them into their pajamas and calmed down enough to catch a few hours of sleep before the big day. As I walked up to Annette's room, I expected to find her jumping on the bed or doing goofy dances on the floor. Instead, I caught a glimpse of her through the door, wiping tears off her face with the sleeve of her nightgown. I walked softly to her and asked, "Annette, why are you so sad? What's the matter?"

"Mommy, I feel so bad inside. I was thinking about tomorrow being Jesus' birthday and about all the things I want for Christmas, and now all I feel is greedy and how bad I am for being so selfish."

Of course, at this point all I wanted to do was make Annette feel better. Of all the impish things my daughter could have been accused of, and that list is very small, being selfish or greedy would not be one of them. Annette had a generous and sensitive spirit. I looked at her innocent face and said, "Annette, you're just excited because there are so many presents under the tree and you have been waiting a long time to open them. Jesus knows that and He is excited for you too. I think it's okay for you to love presents. Jesus is our best present and we love Him. So, why don't we just thank Jesus for all the presents downstairs and for the present that He is to us?" And we did.

Annette's sweet fear of being greedy was not that far off the mark, however. She was experiencing one of her first battles of the flesh. Though we use the word *flesh* to describe the war within, what we are actually saying is that we have a problem with self. Wayne Barber in his book *The Rest of Grace* gives us a simple yet insightful look at how self and flesh share the same meaning. "It is important to keep our terms straight—self and flesh are identical. Sin is the result of self and flesh, and it misses the mark of what God requires. Sin is selfishness, or self-centeredness instead of God-centeredness. Self says, 'I'll do what I want, when I want, how I want.'"[1]

Just as believing with God that our children need Jesus in their lives, we need to believe, really believe with Him, that our children need to live like they have Jesus in their lives. Unless we are in agreement with the Father's heart, we will not fully understand what it means to have a mother's heart. What we believe about salvation and sanctification will be seen in how we share what we believe by living it and teaching it to our children. Our children's growth is important to God.

Forces Without (The World)

My sister has six children and so many grandchildren and more on the way that if I put the number in print, it would change before the ink got dry. As a military family they were always on the move, which gave little opportunity for all the cousins to get together. During a recent visit with my now grown nieces, we sat and reminisced about fun times with our funny family. The girls shared their favorite memory of our son when he was about five years old. "There was Dean," one of them rehearsed, "standing on your picnic table in the backyard with his arms spread out as wide as they would go and singing at the top of his lungs—'I love the world.' He was so cute. Every time we think of Dean, we still see him on that picnic table serenading the world with his song."

Perhaps it's because our children begin their lives with such a simple view of God that spreading out their arms in an offer of praise for the beauty of the world around them pours easily from their childlike hearts. Loving the world with the heart of the Master, however, becomes more difficult the older we get.

The world stands before us like a big blank check offering us a life of unlimited pleasure. It tempts us with all that we want and much that we didn't know we wanted. It disguises our wants as needs and dangles them in front of us. Like a fish to the bait, we swim to the hook and swallow.

We teach our children how to love the world each time we take the bait. This applies not only to the tangible things that money or credit can buy, but to the self-serving and corruptive ways of the world as well. If we want good examples of how corrupted the world is, we need only to sit in our living rooms and watch.

Prime time has fast become the wrong time for kids to be in front of the television. Five minutes of commercials running every eight to ten minutes flashing pretty, tasty, and expensive things in front of them leads them into the world of want. Then during the breaks between commercials coarse language, violence, and sexual innuendoes bombard them. Programs geared toward the younger generation promote a type of lifestyle that God never intended for children of any generation to engage in.

Television alone cannot be blamed for the way the world loves itself. We are self-centered from birth. The world is the place where sin lives. It's like one big pot of self-indulgent, self-gratifying, self-interested flesh. Television didn't create this melting pot of muck; it just re-creates it and feeds it to us in very large portions. This is why the apostle John tells us to not fall in love with the world.

> Don't love the world's ways. Don't love the world's goods. Love of the world squeezes out love for the Father. Practically everything that goes on in the world —wanting your own way, wanting everything for yourself, wanting to appear important—has nothing to do with the Father. It just isolates you from Him. The world and all its wanting, wanting, wanting is on the way out—but whoever does what God wants is set for eternity. (1 John 2:15–17, *The Message*)

When we, as mothers, display a self-indulgent love for the world to our children, we undo all the training in righteousness that we have tried to do. We teach our children by our example that some sin is good. We teach them by our example that we are powerless to resist the ways of the world. And we teach our children by our example that God is a tightwad when it comes to giving us what we need. We teach them everything about the world except the truth.

Our God is neither self-indulgent nor stingy. He loves to lavish us with the best that we need to live happy and holy lives. The world *He* made is full of wonder. But the world He has made has also been corrupted by sin. The only way to love the world is to love it with the Father's heart—full of compassion and pity. The more we observe the Master's heart for the world, the more we will know *how* to give the best to our children without compromising our values or flirting with what the world has to offer us. As we seek to have hearts that are satisfied in Him, they will not find us complaining about what we don't have or lusting over what we shouldn't have. Instead, our children will learn to be thankful receivers, cheerful givers, and strong resisters of life's self-indulgences.

My friend Maria lives in the inner city of Portland. Her neighbors not only keep their doors locked morning, noon, and night, they have iron bars over their doors and windows. Their drapes remain closed even in the daylight hours. Drugs, drive-by shootings, and gangs gathering on the corners is just the way their world is all the time. Many would think that if Maria and her husband, Charles, loved their family they would move. But they, as a family, have a heart for their neighborhood. Their home is a place where lonely kids can come and feel like they belong somewhere. Maria's family rarely throws anything away. Whatever they are finished using they pass on to someone else. They pray earnestly for their neighbors. When a neighbor is sick or discouraged, Maria's family comes quickly to their aid. The hearts of their children are tender to the gospel because they have seen what happens when the world becomes enslaved to sin. As Maria and her family extend their hands to their world with the love of the Father's heart all God's angels sing, "It is good."

The Impostor

While shopping in a Christian bookstore for a Mother's Day gift a few years ago, I found a plaque with a verse written on it. My eye was quickly drawn to its elegant craftsmanship. But when I read the words inscribed on the parchment, the little gift lost its attraction. It said, "God couldn't be everywhere, so He made mothers." Boy, that was a shocker because up until then I was really counting on God being everywhere. As a mother of grown children I knew there was no way I could follow my kids around everywhere they went. They just wouldn't allow it.

Aside from the fact that the silly saying was just plain wrong, it was telling me that I was more omnipresent than God was. What was this thought doing in a Christian bookstore? Wouldn't the Impostor just love for me to think that I can go where God can't?

The leader of the flesh and the world reigns over sin. He watches the ways of the flesh and the world and rejoices over how his influence has infiltrated everything. The Impostor, however, is not omnipresent. He cannot be everywhere, so he polluted the world and the flesh so we would not be able to escape his dominion.

God created mothers so He could reveal His Father's heart to us, and we could share the wonderful world of raising our children together with Him. With our heart in His, we can walk through the experiences we have with our children and see how God has been raising us.

WINDOW TO THE FATHER'S HEART

As I have learned to interact with God concerning my experiences as a mother, He shares with me what being *my* Father is like for Him.

When I say:	**God says:**
Father, do You know what it feels like to have Your child need You so desperately every moment of the day?	Yes, dear one, I do.
Father, do You know what it feels like to have Your child constantly challenge Your wisdom and authority?	Oh, more times than you would know.
Father, do You know what it feels like to have Your child nestle in Your arms while it falls peacefully to sleep?	Yes. Isn't it wonderful to know that your child trusts you enough to sleep confidently through the night?
Father, do You know what it feels like when You see Your child willingly obey You?	I have recorded every marvelous moment down in My Book of Life.
Father, do You know what it feels like to see Your child in pain?	I have a bottle full of her tears.
Father, do You know what it feels like to have Your child turn its back on You?	Oh, the pain is great, isn't it? That's why I stay close to her so I can catch her when she falls.

WHEN I SAY:	GOD SAYS:
Father, do You know what it feels like to see Your child grow up and not need You anymore?	I grew her up on purpose so she would need Me differently.
Father, do You know what it feels like to watch others hurt Your child?	I have, and I have set aside a time to punish the one who is truly responsible.
Father, do You know how it feels to watch Your child succeed?	I call all of heaven to sing for joy when that happens. It's glorious—I can't wait for you to hear it.
Father, do You know what it's like to have Your child bring you a bouquet of dandelions?	They are My greatest treasures. I've been weaving them into a crown.
Father, do You know what it is like to have Your child say "I'm sorry" for the same silly things over and over again?	Oh, my yes, and I love the look on her face when she feels forgiven every single time.
Father, do You know how wonderful it is to be a mom?	Yes, dear one, I do.

When your children see the tender relationship you have with your Master, they will see that God has made their mother's relationship to be a lot like His. "It is good."

3. A SUBMISSIVE HEART

Submission can be a scary word for many women today. It dredges up pictures of forced subservience and mindless obedience that can leave them feeling like being a woman means that they are the lesser of the two sexes. This deceptive picture of submission drawn by the Impostor needs a big eraser taken to it.

There is a lovelier picture of submission, however, that can be illustrated through the bow of a violin. As the maestro gently strokes the bow across the strings of his instrument, a symphony of music fills the air. The bow moves in harmony with the will of the maestro and together they produce the song that would otherwise remain hidden within his heart. The creation of the violin is useless without the agility of the bow in the hand of its master. Likewise, the nature of a woman has been designed to produce the music of a life that is finely tuned to the will of her Musician.

The submissive heart is a heart that chooses to accept the design of her Creator rather than to create the design herself. It is an act of reverence, not to be flaunted, but to be cherished.

It must have been a captivating scene to watch the Master in the Garden fashioning Adam and Eve with His own hands. . Everything else He made was created by the command of His words, but man was sculptured out of clay and woman out of the bone of man. How personal and how tender His touch must have been. The magnificence of my conception compels me to come and worship the One who formed me and to surrender myself fully to Him. With this picture in my mind, I can neither praise myself for the joy I find in being a woman, nor can I will to be something other than what I am. The

work of God's hands as He sculptured me, and the purpose
for which I have been made "is very good."

Look with me and see yourself as you have been designed
by the Master.

The Body's Design

Everything about us is life giving. Whether we have given
birth or whether or not we are able to give birth, we are life
givers. Our bodies are designed for life. This includes our
physical being, our hormonal composition, our emotional
makeup, and our intellectual capabilities.

The female body is designed to conceive, house, bring
forth, and feed another human being; it is a miracle. The
amazing process of pregnancy, I believe, proves that God
exists. Who else could have designed a body to behave in
such a way as this? It is perhaps the most sacrificial act in a
woman's life, one person carrying another person to safety.
The bodies we possess are vehicles for life.

The Heart's Design

We have hearts that are created with the capacity to be
tender to the needs of creatures both great and small. A short
time ago, my husband and I heard the blood-curdling
screams of an injured child outside our home. We both
dashed outside to find a six-year-old boy named Dennis who
had taken a bad spill on his bike. I intuitively wrapped my
arms around him to give him a sense of safety before access-
ing the extent of his cuts and bruises. It wasn't long before his
dad arrived on the scene. The two men were all thumbs when
it came to holding the little guy together, but they were fully
in their element while making plans to transport him to the

hospital. Each one did what they were wired to do. God designed mothers and fathers with different wiring systems so that we can together reflect more fully the nature of God to our children.

The heart of a child finds safety and a place of refuge when nestled securely in its mother's arms. Those moments demonstrate what unconditional love feels like. The child that is carefully nurtured by its mother will grow a well-cared-for soul. A well-cared-for soul will be better prepared to face life, to form healthy relationships, to accept authority, and to live peaceably. We are wired for this very purpose.

The Mind's Design

Cindy is the mother of four fascinating daughters. One day while visiting with her in her home, her two-year-old daughter came into the kitchen to ask for a drink of water. I hadn't noticed how whiny Emily's voice was, but Cindy did. "Emily, ask me in your real voice, please, and I will give you a glass of water." As I watched the interplay between Emily and her mother, I secretly thought Cindy's expectations of a two-year-old were a little too high. Then I heard the most amazing thing. The little girl who came in saying, "Mommeeee, I want thum waduuuu," in a high nasal tone, suddenly looked at her mother and said, "Mommy, can I have some water please?" Cindy's expectations weren't too high at all. She just knew her child.

Mothering is not for dummies. It takes brains and well-trained intuition to raise a child. If we aren't smart they will outsmart us at every turn. By God's design, we mothers have the built-in ability to see the lie in our children's eyes, to hear the cry in their voice, or to sense their fear when they set out on new adventures. It is this quality that will also pierce our hearts as we watch them head toward paths that might lead to their own destruction.

When Cindy listened to the sound of her toddler's voice, she heard the sound of sweet, controlling manipulation. Her gentle correction, brilliantly executed, helped to stop a sin habit before it had time to burrow its roots deep into the behavior of her daughter.

When our minds are filled with the principles of God's Word, we will be able to better see our children from a biblical perspective. This, I believe, is why the Book of Proverbs was written. All of the counsel for rearing children in this book of wisdom can be summed in one verse. "Train a child in the way he should go, and when he is old he will not turn from it" (Proverbs 22:6). Do you need to learn how to raise a child? Read the book and apply it to yourself and to your children. Though they may not always look like they are grateful for its instruction, they will not be able to forget its principles.

When we submit ourselves to the Master's design, we will be free to accept the responsibilities that accompany that design. This may mean tasks like cooking, cleaning, reading to our children, taking walks in the park, praying with them, transporting them to and from their activities, bandaging their knees, and hearing their stories about butterflies in the backyard. These will sometimes place some new demands on our time and patience. But when we collapse in the chair at night, knowing that we have surrendered our heart to the Father's heart, His words of approval make the joys of motherhood a rich reward. "It is good."

4. A SACRIFICIAL HEART

I heard a true and moving story one day on the radio about a mother and her young son who were buried beneath a fallen building for eight days following an earthquake. With no food or water, this poor woman fought for survival. After a few days, it became obvious that the best she could hope was for her precious son to live. At the sacrifice of her own life, she repeatedly pricked her finger, allowing her child to nourish himself from the only thing she could give him, her blood. Eventually the two were found beneath the rubble of the home where they had once lived. Her son survived.

When our children climb into our laps with curly wet hair, smelling all powdery from their bath, and feeling soft and snuggly in their fleece pajamas, we can't help but hold on to them for dear life. Having been attached to them before they were born, the thought of cutting the cord and sending them out on their own can be more than our mother's hearts can bear. But all of us at some point in time will have to say good-bye to our children.

One day while cleaning the walls in our upstairs hallway, I was saddened by how few fingerprints were there to wipe away. I reflected back to the many times when I had grumbled to my family about what their dirty hands were doing to my clean walls. Now I would be thrilled to find just a smudge to mark the territory of where my kids have been. My nest is empty, but my heart is full. I have fingerprints that can never be erased to prove that they have made a lasting imprint in the home of my heart.

Is there anything too great to give up for the sake of a child? Careers, fine clothing, beautiful furniture, a new car, or a degree; can any of these leave fingerprints on our walls? The question should not be, "how much is too much to give?" but "how much is needful?"

The Impostor loves to consume our thoughts with concerns that maybe we are doing too much for our children. Psychology books are full of warnings about taking care of you, not giving in to the trap of codependency, and following the voice of your inner child who needs to be nurtured. Though there may be elements of truth to his warnings, the lies he has perpetrated have nearly succeeded in severing our hearts from our children.

The Master has never asked us to question ourselves regarding how much we are doing for our children. He does, however, pose a similar question to us that we need to take seriously if we are to follow the pattern of His heart. He asks us, "How much is needful?"

As our family was leaving the Portland Coliseum after an evening's entertainment by Mickey Mouse and Donald Duck on ice skates, our kids were so tired that they were nearly asleep on their feet. Without a second's hesitation Dean crawled up my side, wrapped his legs around my waist, his arms around my neck, and headed off to dreamland. Bud spun around, pointed his finger at Dean and said, "Dean, get off your mother. You are too big to be carried. Now stand on your feet and walk like the rest of us."

I hadn't realized until Bud scolded him that night that I had been carrying my baby around way beyond the time that it was needful. When God asks us *how much is needful* He extends to us His care for our well-being as mothers and His wise council for the maturity of our children. Sacrifice given *wisely* will bless our hearts and our children's lives as well.

A mother's heart is a heart that responds to the Master's

sacrificial love by looking at the needs of her children and saying, "My life for yours." There are those who will tell us that we give too much. Yet, a look at the Father's heart reminds us that a child is worth the cost. He will give us the courage to stand firm against their words, and declare boldly, "Step aside, I have needs to meet, and promises to keep, and futures that need my attention."

How will our children know the value of Christ's sacrifice if we don't model it for them? "It is good."

5. A HOPEFUL HEART

It can be a terrifying responsibility to be a mom! What if your mistakes and your inadequacies cause your children to become the world's next great terrorists? What if the circumstances in your home lead your children into a future of unrestrained chaos?

I have found incredible comfort in knowing that God never wrings His holy hands over the rebellious turns my children and I take from time to time. Just as I see that His love bears all things and believes all things, I see that His love also *hopes* all things. His omniscient love, which knows the beginning and the end of our lives, removes the fear I might otherwise have for the future.

Hope is a characteristic that beautifies God's women! It keeps our faces from becoming hardened by bitterness and fear. When we are women with saved, sanctified, submitted and sacrificial hearts we will know that we can trust our omnipotent, omniscient, and omnipresent God with the future of our children.

My hope for my children goes beyond any short-term goals I might have for them. Though I pray for their daily success, I want them to live lives that will not bring dishonor to God's reputation. My hope for my children is that by the end of their lives they will have become shining reflections of the Master. He knows the plans He has for them. His plans will insure their futures and give them hope for their own lives. When my desire for them lines up with His, I can yield their lives into His hands with confidence and hopeful expectation.

Hope is exercised through and accompanied by prayer. Motherhood is more about prayer than it is about performance. Prayer precedes performance. Prayer inspires performance. Prayer perfects performance. Sending our children out the door without prayer is like tossing them out into the snow without a coat.

I have known many good parents whose children have taken a detour through life. The pain of a child's rebellion can often leave their parents feeling as if they will never be able to survive the pain. They write mental lists of the mistakes they made hoping to find a good reason for their children's refusal to live godly lives. They often lay awake at night wondering where the time spent in prayer, council, fellowship, and spiritual nurturing went. Some question their faith and the power of God. Perhaps these needy parents understand hope better than the parents who have never walked in their shoes do.

Hope that is *seen* is no hope at all. Hope is confidence in what is not seen. This confidence assures us that God will not abandon our children, no matter how grim their ungodly rebellion may appear to be.

A mother who has a hopeful heart has a more perfect view of the Master's love for her and her children. "It is good."

6. A PEACEFUL HEART

I sat on the couch one morning gazing into the fog. My heart felt as heavy as the thick gray cloud that enveloped our neighborhood. *Oh, God, I feel so barren today. Life is as bleak for me right now as this fog into which I am staring. Why don't You come and take it all away? I'm tired of feeling tired, and my soul is more troubled within me than I can even bear to express.*

Time passed slowly that morning. I have no idea how long I remained with my stare fixed into the fog, but I remember distinctly the peace that slowly released me from my depression. It came gently as the clouds lifted, revealing the houses and the lawns and the dogs barking at the garbage man. Everything was as it had been before the fog descended.

We all feel like failures at times. Thoughts of what we should have done and the things we wish we hadn't done will roll over us like a heavy blanket of gloom. Peace is the refreshment that comes when God lifts us to a place where we can see beyond the fog. It is there we discover the comfort of our Father's heart who will never leave us and where we receive rest for our weary souls. Through all the experiences of motherhood, the Master is writing our story into *His*-story. He is writing the story of our children's lives as well. We may not know what's ahead for ourselves or for our children; but take courage, the final chapter has been written and it closes with victory, for all return to the Father's heart. "It is good."

A FRESH START FOR A NEW HEART

Before we can make a fresh start as mothers, we must first turn toward the enemy of our hearts, hold up our shield before him, and say no to all that would distract us from developing hearts that are saved, sanctified, submissive, sacrificial, hopeful, and peaceful. A daily look at the condition of our heart is needed in order to win the battle against the Impostor.

These six essential qualities of the Father's heart are available to us upon request. When the Impostor seeks to draw our hearts away from our children, we can look into our Father's heart and know what we need to do. Rebel. Say no. Run back to our children, hold them close and love them with all that has been given to us when God created us for motherhood. "It is very, very good."

The Call of the Imposter

I was there when you were fashioned to be the lovely creature that you are. I put passion in your heart. You are destined to do great things. Has not the Master designed you for this? Time is your enemy. I want you to experience it all. Motherhood will not satisfy your longings unless you first meet the needs of your own personhood. Do you want what is best for your children? So do I! Listen then to what I say. I desire true freedom for your life. I want you to be praised, by your children, by your husband, by your church, but most of all by you yourself. So be praiseworthy. You are the pacesetter for your children's lives. How will your children know the way unless you show it to them? If you are not happy, you will raise unhappy children. Any sense of inadequacy that you feel is merely the residue of antiquated teachings. You are eternal! Now go and teach others what true spiritual mothering really is! Lead them out of their bondage! Raise up an army of freedom fighters. Go and win the battle!

The Call of the Master

There is a way that seems right, but if you follow that way you will come to destruction, and you will lead your children to follow you right into the enemy's snare. I have created life, and I have created you to be a life-giver. The beauty of how I created you has given you the ability to procreate beauty. The little ones I have given you are My gift to you. I loved them before you knew them. They are also Mine. We are in partnership in this process of parenting. You will hear many voices crying out to you that you are losing yourself as you raise these little ones that have been put under your charge. But I say to you, how will you lose what you have not *yourself* created? Love your children the way I love you, and trust Me to do the rest. I am your hope, and I am your peace. We will laugh and cry together during these years of mothering. Seek Me, speak to Me, trust Me, grow in Me, and listen to what I tell you in My Word. You are My design. Now stand firm and face the Impostor. Put out your hand as a shield and shout, "No more!" Draw the line in the sand. This is the rebellion that pleases Me. Keep focused on the goal. You will find joy as a mother that will be greater than anything you can create for yourself. Enjoy their hugs, the bouquets of dandelions they present to you, and the good that dwells in them as evidences of My favor upon your good work. Continue on in faithfulness until that day when I Myself will say to you, "It is good."

The Heart in a Briefcase

The design of all created things is to reflect the glory of God.

GORDON MACDONALD, *THE LIFE GOD BLESSES*

CHAPTER SEVEN

Oh God, I'm perpetually praying on the run
My kids are forever in need
My husband can't find his socks
I barely make it to work on time
Then I rush through the day
Hoping to get home on time
Hurry through dinner
Get caught up on the wash
Slap a goodnight kiss on my children's faces
I steal away to the living room for a few precious moments
At last I am alone.
Then he comes in and smiles that smile....
My thoughts turn evil
"Tonight? Are you nuts?"
By the time my head sinks into my pillow
I whisper a quick few words to You
But before I get to the important stuff,
I fall asleep
My life consists of rushing through today
So I can charge into tomorrow
And where are You, God?
In the midst of the chaos,
Where are You?

SANDY SNAVELY

*C*limbing the corporate ladder in heels can be hazardous, especially if your career isn't the only thing in your life that's important to you.

If it weren't for all the added responsibilities heaped upon the working woman of today, she would be free to become all that she can be. Instead, the needs of her children, husband, dog, cat, home, and friends stand in her way as she pounds her fists against the glass ceiling. None of it seems *fair,* but as she has learned from the world around her, *fair* is not always a privilege of the female gender. Her passionate determination to succeed lives in defiant opposition to her quiet longing for the smell of lavender and a desire to stand still and treasure the soft touch of a baby's hand on her face.

I understand the frustration of trying to balance two worlds that are often unsympathetic toward each other. When it seems that no one else understands the pressures of the working woman, there is a comforting togetherness to be found within the cluster of those who see themselves as victims of their inequitable responsibilities. The truth, however, is that we are more frequently hostages of our own Type A personalities than helpless underdogs in the personnel office of opportunity.

I had no idea what a driven woman I was until I joined the ranks of the working woman. I waited until my children were grown before I began a career that evolved from business, to broadcasting, and then—retirement. Even though our children were no longer dependent on me to be their stay-at-home mommy, I still could not escape the feeling that I was driving east in the westbound lane of traffic. Was I wrong to go to work? Didn't I have the right to do what I wanted now that I had done what was expected of me? I was filled with questions, and there were plenty of self-proclaimed prophets eager to encourage, discourage, and enlighten me about the changing roles of today's woman. But the voice I needed to hear most seemed strangely silent. It wasn't until I began to ask the right question that I found the Master's wisdom scrolled across the pages of my day planner.

TO WORK OR NOT TO WORK— THIS IS NOT THE QUESTION!

As a student in business school, Kelly had big dreams and grand visions. On her first day of class, she came dressed in a business suit carrying a briefcase crafted in fine leather with shiny brass accessories. Kelly looked the part of a young professional bound for success. There was one problem, however, that blasted her image right off the pages of *Fortune 500*. With the exception of a legal pad and a ballpoint pen, her briefcase was empty.

Of course, Kelly was young and impressionable. Her aspirations were much higher at that point than her accomplishments. And there is some truth to the old adage that if you want to be successful you have to look and act the part. Yet the empty briefcase that Kelly carried with such pride and pretension defines the hearts of many working women today. The thing that might often be the evidence of our success reveals instead the emptiness of it.

In our society, where image is everything, women who work are often pitted against women who don't. Unfortunately, the hostility between these two groups isn't just limited to the world's battlefields. Instead, both men and women in the church can just as easily be found taking up sides in the debate and drawing their lines in the sand with arrogant pride while the Impostor dances to the tune of our philosophical gunfire. The typical topics run amuck as the *Militant Should Work,* the *Defenseless Must Work,* and the *Spiritual Wouldn't Dare Work Because It's Not What Good Christian Women Do* have a not so spiritual slugfest over who is on the better side of right.

We are God's chosen women, and therefore, we have only one legitimate side in this debate to choose—His! As we have been discovering, what we do as women matters to God. Our lives as His women whether as homemakers, as wives, or as mothers are of great concern to Him. But the world outside of our home is also of great concern to Him. God is neither for nor against the working woman. He is for the plans He has prepared for the women of His heart. Therefore, where we fit in our homes and in the world cannot be discovered until we come into His heart and let Him show us *our* lives from His perspective.

If we are women who want the Master's seal of approval on all we do, we must be willing to have our minds changed regarding how we see ourselves and other women who work outside the home. The real question for us, perhaps, is this: Are we willing to see our lives from God's perspective and to agree with His plan for our lives? How God answers this question might well be different for me than it is for you. It might be that God would choose to tell you to go back home for a season and then to reenter the workplace when the current priorities of His heart have been fulfilled. It may be that you will discover that you are never to work outside the home. If we trust that God is omniscient, that He knows everything about us—our needs, our dreams, our fields of interest, our skills, and our priorities—we can come to Him without fearing His answer. If we trust that God is omnipresent, always with us everywhere we go, we can trust that He will be with us in the decisions that we need to make. And if we believe that God is omnipotent, thoroughly powerful and fully able, we can trust that He has the power to care for us and meet our needs wherever His decision takes us.

Throughout this chapter I refer to the briefcase, but not because I believe that all women are destined to enter the business world where briefcases are a typical part of their attire. Instead, I have chosen this to symbolize the way we see our jobs in light of our worth and value. There is nothing more futile in a woman's life than to carry around an empty briefcase giving off airs of self-imposed importance while we stand before the Master with our true treasures exposed for all of heaven to see.

> It's obvious, isn't it? The place where your treasure is,
> is the place you will most want to be, and end up
> being. (Matthew 6:21, *The Message*)

The questions that need to be addressed may be uncomfortably personal: "Why do *you* work?" and "Should *you* work?"

WHY *VS.* SHOULD: THE COLLISION COURSE OF CONSCIENCE

While I believe it is harmful for those of us in the household of the Master to impose guilt upon each other for why we do or do not work outside the home, I do believe that there is legitimate guilt we need to face individually regarding this issue. There is a right cause for our consciences to be in conflict if we are in a place where we should not be. If our souls become agitated over the "why vs. should" issue in our lives, then this is the most important place for us to start if we want our lives to be in comfortable alignment with the Master's heart.

These two questions are critical to our well-being as working women. They have proven very crucial to me. Though now retired, I work at home. Every day, I spend several hours away from my husband putting words into a computer, deleting words from the computer, and rewriting them again—Mr. P.C. is a merciless boss. Working outside the home, working inside the home, or serving in other capacities that divert our attention away from the home all have the potential to put our priorities to the test.

Home, so we've seen, is the heartbeat of the Master and the pulse of society. Every news item and every event in human history has had its beginnings in the home. Whether or not we are married, single, married with children or married without children, divorced or widowed, home is our first priority. It is by God's design that He has called us as women to be first and foremost—home-centered.

The conflict of conscience will always rage within us when our hearts are wandering in a different direction than His. If we want to stay on track with Him and defeat the Impostor in our lives, we must be willing to lift the lid of our proverbial briefcases and allow the Master to fill them with His wisdom and direction. If you were to invite Him to sort through the secret files of your heart where your reasons for working are contained, what confessions would He find hiding inside?

I work because:

- I am the only able-bodied financial provider in my home.
- I have skills that need to be kept current in today's marketplace.
- I need the sense of self-esteem and empowerment that my career provides.
- I can't stand being with my children all day, every day.
- My children don't need me at home anymore.
- I love the independence of having my own income.
- I am proud of the position I have in the marketplace.
- My husband has been financially irresponsible.
- I need to help my children have the things they need in life.
- I am helping my children go to college.
- My husband needs to finish his education.
- Women who don't work are less valued in today's society.
- The cost of living requires a dual income just to survive.
- God has called me to be His ambassador in the marketplace.
- I am in full-time ministry.
- I don't know how to stay home.
- I need to.
- I want to.

These are just eighteen reasons *why* you might be working outside of your home. Facing them head-on will either cause you to cringe at the truth, to get angry with me for speaking it so bluntly, or to feel the peace that comes through a God-approved conscience. In any case, you can be sure of one thing—God has a plan for your life. Though you may need to change the course you are on, readjust your motives, or praise God for where He has put you, your life is valuable to the Master. I would encourage you to go over this list one more time and hold each reason under the light of the Scripture we will be focusing on throughout this chapter.

> For where your treasure is, there your heart will be also. (Matthew 6:21)

If you are on a collision course of conscience, it might well be because you are currently caught between the *why* and the *should* in your career plans. Many of us may feel like we have good reasons for doing what we do, but none of them will survive our explanations if they aren't backed up by a really good *should*.

> But you are a chosen people, a royal priesthood, a holy nation, a people belonging to God, that you may declare the praises of him who called you out of darkness into his wonderful light. (1 Peter 2:9)

Let's see what wisdom an Old Testament priest has to contribute to our dilemma.

INQUIRING MINDS WANT TO KNOW

When the Old Testament priesthood first began through Aaron, the brother of Moses, God gave some very specific instructions as to how the priesthood of Israel was to be ordered. From the building of the tabernacle to the furnishings and even the clothing worn by the priestly line, all things were designed with deep symbolic meaning. Perhaps the most mysterious symbolism found among the holy garments for the high priest was the Urim and Thummim held in the breastpiece of decision which was worn over the priest's heart. Not a lot is known about the Urim and Thummim except that the words mean "curses and perfections," and they were used as sacred lots to determine the will of God in times of crisis. What was clear, however, was that man's wisdom, even the wisdom of a high priest, was inadequate and subject to the corruption of the flesh. The wisdom of God was given through the priest who held the Urim and Thummim over his heart so that God alone could rule over the affairs of His people.

Where are the Urim and Thummim today? God has declared that we who know Christ are both His chosen women and His royal priesthood. His wisdom not only covers our hearts but it flows from within our hearts through the in-dwelling presence of the Holy Spirit—in a sense, our Urim and Thummim—Who will guide us in the right direction.

Worldly rhetoric, Sunday school answers, and legalistic judgements are a poor substitute for the voice of God leading us in the direction in which He has ordained for us to go. "Who *should* work?" is a serious question, and it deserves the highest wisdom to determine the answer. I don't have any answers, but I can open up my briefcase and share the wisdom God has given me through the successes and failures I have experienced having been both a stay-at-home mom and a working woman.

CONFESSIONS OF A WORKING WOMAN

I am an over-achiever. I want to leave my mark on the world. I want to do something that will count for eternity. I was born with my hand up ready to volunteer almost before I took my first breath. My answers for why *I* went to work are all wrapped into the reality of these confessions. Basically, I saw working outside the home as a means to fulfill the burning desire in my heart to do something big.

Beginning at a sales counter in a jewelry store, I was promoted quickly through the ranks until I became a company supervisor. My experience in retail prepared me for a move into marketing where I took a position as a marketing director for a local shopping center. From there I was hired to purchase and market products for a chain of Christian bookstores which in turn led me to a Christian radio station to be a talk show host. My career has been a carnival ride through exciting experiences and challenging responsibilities.

When I began working outside the home, I felt a bit snobbish about my well-ordered life. I had done it all just right. I had stayed home and raised my children before I ventured out the door to do my own thing. I was very proud of myself.

Yet, as charmed as I was regarding my integrity as a mother, I forgot that I had a husband at home who was not ready to outgrow his need of a wife. Bud was unprepared for the long hours that were required of me as I fought my way up the ladder of success. His well-being was often sacrificed for fourteen-hour days that made me the little darling in my boss's eyes but a long lost friend to my husband.

Who Should Work?

To my surprise, I discovered that this question is not only pertinent to the mother with children at home, but to the woman who is married to a man who loves his wife and needs to be her number one priority.

Perhaps the answer is more easily found in the heart of *why* we are leaving our home to go to work. If the drive within to conquer new worlds is greater than the needs of the people around us, maybe we are not being called to circulate a fashionable résumé. Some adjustments to our schedules just might be in order.

What Kind of Work Should She Do?

While tending to a promotion in the mall where I was the marketer, a young marketing wanna-be came to me with stars in his eyes and said, "Wow, what a great job you have."

My response to his comment was more convicting to me than it was to him: "If you want a job that encourages people to spend money so they will have to go out and make more money so they can come in again and spend money, then I guess you are right. This is a great job."

There certainly is nothing morally wrong with being a marketing director unless you are consumed with a competitive spirit that drives you to want more, have more, and be more. While working at the mall, I had allowed myself to get caught up in the success, power, and money trap. The clients I rubbed shoulders with admired me. I loved the prestige that was a part of my decision-making responsibilities. I loved the title on my business cards. When this young man came to me, looking like a puppy in a dog food store, God used my own words to call me back to His heart and to reexamine the motives I had for my career.

What a woman does when she goes to work has the potential to grow her as a woman of the Master's heart or draw her into the Impostor's world of fuzzy ethics, inflated egos, misplaced priorities, and temporal pleasures.

> Do nothing from selfishness or empty conceit, but with humility of mind let each of you regard one another as more important than himself; do not merely look out for your own personal interests, but also for the interests of others. (Philippians 2:3–4, NASB)

When Should a Woman Go to Work?

> There is a time for everything, and a season for every activity under heaven. (Ecclesiastes 3:1)

What time is it on your woman's watch? When I was a young woman, I feared that life would fly past me while I was folding diapers and wiping noses. I had dreams and ambitions that I longed to fulfill. I worried that by the time I was free to launch into the workforce I would be outdated and unmarketable. What I found instead was that the exact opposite was true. My years of managing a home and raising children gave me an edge of maturity that was lacking in many of the women who were younger than I. The time I spent completing my God given assignments at home were valuable preparation for everything I have been doing since. No time is ever wasted on the Master's timecard.

When our son, Dean, was a junior in high school, I took a part-time job in a deli. Somehow it seemed that feeding strangers was more challenging than feeding my family, so I put on my apron and went to work. Everything was going well until the enemy of the working mother came knocking on the door and introduced himself to me, "Hello, I'm Summer Vacation!" One hot August day after I had just gotten home from a hard afternoon of pickle diving, Dean had one of his infamous thirty-second heart-to-hearts with Mom. "I hate your job. I like having you home. This place is lonely." I quit my job and resumed my full-time career as a wife and mother. The following year, Dean sat me down for another in-depth meeting of the minds. "If you want to go to work, it's really okay with me. I don't need you at home anymore." What a difference a year made.

When we go to work has everything to do with God's plan for our lives. *When* we have completed our current assignments, we can be sure that the experiences gained will prepare us for the next task. Whatever is in His mind for us to do will be waiting for us, *when* He calls us to go and do it. God never stands in front of us tapping His foot and pointing to His watch trying to hurry us through the various seasons of our lives. Instead, He treasures each one and desires for us to treasure them with Him.

Where Should I Be Right Now?

The best place to be today is right where you are. I am convinced that if we are running in search of where we need to be, we will not be still when the Master speaks. Being still is the only way we will know where He desires to place us.

While working in a chain of Christian bookstores, I had a suspicion that I was about to be fired. The company I was working for was going through a time of intense internal turmoil, and I was caught in the middle of it. I had never in my other jobs been given less than an excellent review, thus the prospect of being handed a pink slip made me weak in the knees. First, I fumbled around looking for a new position where my skills would be significant and respected. But each time a new job was offered to me God's voice preempted my final decision with an unmistakable no. I had already learned by that point to ask God first before making critical life decisions and to obey Him when He gives me the answers. Nevertheless, I couldn't seem to shake the desire to run away from the problem I was facing at work.

One day on the way to my office I cried out to God asking Him to direct my steps to where He wanted me to be so that I could do what He wanted me to do. His voice spoke simply and quietly to my soul.

> He has showed you, O [woman], what is good.
> And what does the LORD require of you?
> To act justly and to love mercy
> and to walk humbly with your God. (Micah 6:8)

How perfect and how wise His words were to me that morning. As an administrator in that company there were many employees who needed daily encouragement and protection while the crisis was brewing. The door to my office was constantly open to hurting hearts. As long as I focused on being there for them, I was able to forsake the fear I had for my own future. But when I would allow panic to seize control of my emotions, my feet would start to run away from the problems that God was calling me to face. My Urim and Thummim were in high gear.

At just the right time, a Christian radio station hired me to host a two-hour a day, five days a week, talk show in the Portland/Vancouver area. I was free to leave my job with dignity and integrity intact. Life couldn't have been better. Someone was actually going to *pay* me to talk!

As the popularity of my show began to build, I knew I was exactly where God wanted me to be. My tenure lasted for five incredible years. Not one day was ever the same as the day before. The challenge was exhilarating, and the experiences prepared me for the day I was called into the conference room where I was told that my program was being cancelled.

Today I am at home learning to be a writer. Again the timing of my Master is perfect. I am right where He wants me to be. His voice always speaks when I am still before Him.

> Whether you turn to the right or to the left, your ears will hear a voice behind you, saying, "This is the way; walk in it." (Isaiah 30:21)

How Shall I Live as His Working Woman?

You shall live the same way as the Master's women who are called to stay at home—in full surrender to Him.

During the first few years that I worked outside of my home, I had the mistaken notion that I was now different than my sisters in Christ who were stay-at-home wives and mothers. My job ate away at the time I used to spend being nurtured by my quiet time with the Master, quality time with my husband, and time fulfilling the responsibility of caring for the needs of my home.

Working became a substitute for serving in the church, serving in my home, and spending time with my friends. I was building a career and leaving everyone I loved behind in the process. God's ways and my ways were opposing each other.

After finding my seat on board a small plane bound for Yakima, Washington, I looked around and discovered that I had become a clone. Women in business suits carrying brief-cases were sitting behind me, next to me, and in front of me. Emotionless pod people on a mission to take over the world had invaded the plane and I was one of them. I had achieved what I had set out to do. I had become a working woman, but I looked more like a working woman patterned after the Impostor's design. My briefcase was empty, and my heart was consumed with misplaced treasures. God's voice thundered in my ears over the roar of the engines of the plane:

It's obvious, isn't it? The place where your treasure is,
is the place you will most want to be, and end up
being. (Matthew 6:21, *The Message*)

What God showed me in the weeks following my trip to Washington changed my life as a working woman. The *who, what, where, when,* and *how* in the lives of working women are to be found in the wisdom of the Master, daily applied to the hearts of those who truly desire to live according to His design. It is this pursuit, both in women who work and women who don't, that will join us together in a common bond of mutual love, respect, and intimate friendship.

Obedience and willing, joyful submission feels good and looks good on the women chosen by the Master to display His character in a sinful world. Full hearts are so much easier to carry than empty briefcases.

My good friend Victoria is a highly respected talk show host. Victoria is bright, well informed, opinionated, and fearless. Her evening talk show became a quick hit with people from many walks of life. Yet the time she spent preparing for her programs and behind of the microphone left her little time to spend with her family. When she was given the dreaded pink slip that sent her back home to be a full-time wife and mother, it was a shock to everyone—especially Victoria. She spent long hours looking for an open spot in a very tight radio market. But she also rediscovered the joys of being home with her children. Her heart was torn between her love for her career and her love for her home. But God was not shocked. He had a better plan for Victoria. Eventually, she landed a three-hour Saturday show on a popular radio station in the Northwest. Her love for family and career are at peace with each other.

In a recent conversation, Victoria shared a precious picture with me that I believe portrays what the woman who is in the right place with her Master looks like. She told me: "I found myself smiling at my daughter the other day as she was telling me what things were on her important schedule. And I heard myself saying, 'I can take you there...I can pick you up for that.' It was such a great feeling to be able to look at her and know that I could really be there for her."

When we are in the right place with the Master, peace is inevitable.

TREASURE HUNTING IN THE SOUL

Don't pile up treasures on earth, where moth and rust can spoil them and thieves can break in and steal. But

keep your treasure in Heaven where there is neither
moth nor rust to spoil it and nobody can break in
and steal. For wherever your treasure is, you may be
certain that your heart will be there too! (Matthew
6:19–21, Phillips)

The woman who seeks truth, no matter what the cost, is the
woman who has learned to be a true treasure hunter. She
knows the difference between worthless junk and timeless
treasures. She loves what the Master loves and hates what the
Impostor loves.

Found among the cobwebs inside the briefcase of a
woman's earthly life, its contents prove where her heart has
been gathering. As she peruses the items inside, the truth of
their value will reveal what she has been running away from.
It might well be:

- She has been working out of sync with the priorities of
  her home and family.
- Her children and husband are paying the price for her
  ambition and success.
- Her church doesn't benefit from the spiritual gifts given
  to her by the Master.
- Her friends are left to the mercy of her busy schedule.
- Important organizations lack her voluntary support.
- Her temperament has become hard, masculine, and
  unrelenting.
- Her vision is bound by her own need for satisfaction.
- She is fearful of losing her status in the marketplace.
- She is fearful of financial failure.
- She is consumed with her need for monetary possessions.

- She doesn't trust her husband's ability to provide for their family.
- Her job is an obstacle to her spiritual growth.
- Her life leaves no eternal value in the marketplace.
- She makes decisions and then asks God to bless them.
- Her troubled conscience exposes that her work does not have the Master's seal of approval.

But the woman who knows her God and walks obediently according to His design for her life will open her briefcase and find her eternal treasures glowing from within:

- Her priorities are in sync with the Master's call on her life.
- Her family rests in her loving care.
- Her spiritual gifts are valuable in her church.
- Her friends trust her love for them.
- She is able to give of her time to others in need.
- Her femininity is enhanced through her kind, loving, generous character.
- Her life is marked by the Master's vision for her life.
- She has no fear for how the world views her priorities.
- She has no fear for her financial future.
- She values what she has without a craving for more.
- She honors her husband's efforts to provide for the needs of their family.
- She has time to be diligent in her desire for spiritual growth.
- Her life has an eternal impact in the marketplace.
- Whether single or married, with or without children at home, God is the driving force of her decisions.

- She has the Master's seal of approval over all she is doing.

A PATH WORTH FINDING

The way to the treasures that last has been already charted for us by the Master's hand. He is eager to show it to us, for He knows that His design will bring us complete fulfillment and eternal joy. The question for His chosen women is, "Will we trust Him to direct our steps or will we allow the Impostor to be our guide?"

God knows your heart. He has created you to do something wonderful in His kingdom. No one else can do it but you because it has been tailor-made according to the gifts He has given you. Whether you are a single woman, a working single mother, a working married mother, a widow, or a wife with grown children, if you are on the right track, your heart will say "yes" and "amen" to His will for your life. If you are not in sync with Him, can you trust Him with the decisions that He is tugging at your heart to make? This promise is for you.

> Thou wilt shew me the path of life:
> in thy presence is fulness of joy;
> at thy right hand there are pleasures for evermore.
> (Psalm 16:11, KJV)

Take a stand against the lies fostered through the world's system by the voice of the Impostor.

> I'm not asking that you take them out of the world
> But that you guard them from the Evil One.

They are no more defined by the world
Than I am defined by the world.
Make them holy—consecrated—with the truth;
Your word is consecrating truth.
In the same way that you gave me a mission in the
world,
I give them a mission in the world.
(John 17:15–18, *The Message*)

The Call of the Imposter

How long will you continue to be torn in two directions because of the lies of those who have small minds and narrow vision? Surely you know that their philosophies are rooted in the past. There was a time when women stayed home, baked cookies, and agonized over how to get the grass stains out of their children's clothes. But this is a new day. Your foremothers who fought for your right to break free from this pitiful mold deserve more respect than this.

I am here to remind you of your worth. I know you are feeling the weight of the guilt imposed on you from the religiously militant homebodies who won't be happy until they corral all women into their way of thinking. What they fail to understand is that the Master's work will not be accomplished if everyone lives the way they do.

You need to work. You were designed for it. Look how successful you are and see the potential that is ahead for you—if you stay on course. The world is a competitive place and you're not getting any younger. You can't afford to waste time with temporal tasks that keep you from your true calling. If your family, friends, and even your church love you, they will give you the space you need to carve out your own destiny and find your own personal fulfillment. Just think of what the world won't have if you shrink back.

That is not just a briefcase you are carrying, it is the identity you have been searching for all your life. In it you will have the power, autonomy, satisfaction, and provision to be what you have always wanted to be—a woman who has it all.

The Call of the Master

Do you know what will be the length of your days? Do you know what will happen tomorrow? Can you look into the future and see what is ahead for you? Is there anything in that briefcase of yours that will help you to answer these simple questions?

Come with Me and see into My heart. My concern is not just for you but for the entire world. The harvest has begun and you have a significant role to play in the gleaning process. My call on your life is for you to be My woman, chosen to be in the place I have designed only for you. Therefore, I have a long-range plan for where you are to be at each unique stage of your life.

I am faithful. Your home is My first priority. I will never lead you in a path that will bring harm to you or to your family. My grace will be sufficient to fill your heart with every good thing that is needed so you can go through your life with a good conscience. Dear one, be assured of this; when you are doing My will, all the people I have put in your life will be rewarded because of your ways of blessing.

There is a time for everything in My kingdom. This is why you must learn to listen for My voice to guide you in all of your life's decisions. The jobs I give to My treasured daughters are all uniquely designed by Me to bring them to full maturity. I give careers that will provide for My children's needs and that will sprinkle My people throughout the world to show the world who I am.

I know the plans that I have for you. I call you today to trust Me with the length of your days. Your clock will not run out of time to do all that is in My heart for you to do. Trust Me. My ways are right and My will is good. Without My vision in the hearts of My people, people will perish. Have My vision and the abundant life you long for will be yours.

The Beautiful Heart

For we are God's workmanship,
created in Christ Jesus to do good works,
which God prepared in advance
for us to do.

EPHESIANS 2:10

CHAPTER EIGHT

*W*hile browsing through some old photographs, I came across a picture of a young woman on a beach. Her face looked familiar. I stared at her for a moment and then recognized the attractive girl running through the waves without a wrinkle on her face. She was me. A momentary wave of sadness swept over my heart as I realized how quickly time had passed and how impartial the aging process had been.

I have had a love/hate relationship with growing old. For so many years I was the youngest woman in Bible study groups and the youngest mother in PTA, and I longed for the credibility that the older women around me seemed to have. On the other hand, I have often been shocked as a look in the mirror revealed my mother's face staring back at me. I guess I hoped that I would grow older and wiser but continue to look younger in the process.

I don't suppose I'm all that different from most women who remember the days when their faces were tight, and they could be seen in public without make-up. Even as I go through what I do to make my face look younger than it really is, there is one face that is alive in my memory to remind me of what true beauty looks like. Hers was one of the most beautiful faces I have ever seen.

I met her in a convalescent home where I had been asked to come to entertain the elderly patients. My colorful wig, big floppy shoes, and red rubber nose stood in stark contrast to the cruel consequences of growing old. There in one of the rooms was the woman who would redefine my definition of beauty.

Her frail body lay imprisoned by the bars of a hospital bed. Long strands of snow-white hair webbed across the cotton pillow that cradled her head. Ivory skin clung tightly to her perfect cheekbones and delicate chin. When I came near, the woman's slender fingers pulled my face close to hers. The gentleness of her soul shone through her clear blue eyes. Her beauty captivated me. With my ear close to her lips she sang to me the finale of her life's story. *"Jesus, Jesus, oh, how I love Him."*

There was a sweet boldness to her words. I felt small standing next to her in my silly disguise. I thought I was there to bring joy to people whose lives were nearing an end. Instead she brought joy to mine.

Her words were sung as a testimony to the loveliness of this woman's heart inside a body that was quickly withering away. Without knowing it, she left a legacy of beauty that continues to sing its quiet message to me. While photographs record the visible story of our lives, our hearts carry the message of our substance. Perhaps one day when my children thumb through our family albums, they will see beyond the aging face of their mother in the pictures and say, "That was a beautiful woman."

OUTWARD BEAUTY—IMPOSTOR STYLE

Every year Hollywood commemorates the untimely death of Marilynn Monroe, the blond bombshell of the movie screen.

I wonder now and then what she would have looked like today had she lived to be a senior citizen. Would she have been willing to grow old gracefully like my friend in the convalescent home or would she, like thousands of other women, have spent her fortune on plastic surgeons trying to keep the truth from staring at her in her mirror?

Vanity. Everywhere we turn we are faced with a culture obsessed with youth. Models just barely old enough to put their acne creams away swoosh their hair across the screen displaying how their product gets rid of gray hair, as if they had gray hair! Couldn't they find a woman who actually had gray hair? Of course, that would mean they would have to hire someone who is—old.

Vanity. We're a culture obsessed with fashion. Tall skinny models that haven't eaten in years parade themselves in front of us promising that we can look just like them if we can squeeze into what they are wearing.

Vanity. Everywhere we turn we're faced with a culture that is obsessed with beauty. Lipsticks that promise not to smudge off while you're kissing, mascara that makes your lashes look six feet long and toothpaste that makes your teeth glow in the dark, line the cosmetic shelves.

Solomon was right. Our lives are full of vanity.

"Meaningless! Meaningless!" says the Teacher. "Everything is meaningless!" Now all has been heard; here is the conclusion of the matter: Fear God and keep his commandments, for this is the whole duty of man. For God will bring every deed into judgment, including every hidden thing, whether it is good or evil. (Ecclesiastes 12:8, 13–14)

234 CALLED TO REBELLION

Life, as Solomon observed, is empty, futile, worthless, meaningless, useless, hollow, purposeless, and a waste of our time. No matter what we do to make it look better than it is, there is nothing we can do to change the fact that without God, life is utterly intolerable. The best we can hope for, if we choose to leave God out of the picture, is to paint over the truth with pretty colors and fine things so we won't have to endure the emptiness of our own existence.

People have been using outward beauty to cover their dark side since the beginning of sin. We do this because we are vain. Vanity, as paraphrased from the three dictionaries on my desk, is an excessive concern for our outward appearance or our inward value. The desire for outward beauty is a type of vanity that can cause us to be overly concerned with how we look so that we can feel better about who we are. Beauty the Impostor's way keeps us from facing the truth; without God we are unsightly, ill-favored, purposeless people.

Beauty is what caused Samson to lose his sight. It is what led Ahab to subcontract his kingly power to his beautiful but wicked wife Jezebel. And beauty bears the blame for delivering John the Baptist's head on a platter to Herod so he could watch his beautiful stepdaughter Salome dance.

Though some people may point the finger at Hollywood for fostering our nation's addiction to beauty, it just might be possible that they deserve an award for their accurate portrayal of what human nature has been like ever since we first learned to say, "Wow!"

The desire for outward beauty is one of the strongest drives that continues to submerge our culture deeper and deeper into the abyss of sensual pleasures and addictive materialism. Beauty in the Impostor's style is an aphrodisiac for the ego.

Because he cannot create beauty he has become a genius at redefining it and selling it to us for no small amount of our hard-earned money.

His type of beauty is what has inspired fashion trends from before Cleopatra to after Cindy Crawford. The renaissance women of old who made cellulite enviable, the emaciated figure of Twiggy, long flowing hair, short crew cuts, French nails—all are figments of his vain imagination. He doesn't have the capacity to make beauty happen, so he has become a redesigner of beauty.

The Impostor's approach to beauty is based on one simple principle; decorate the closet door and toss the ugly stuff inside. As he succeeds in creating a false illusion of who we are, established by what we look like, he then succeeds in keeping us off the track that leads to true lasting beauty. His way to beauty will never lead us to the Master's heart.

OUTWARD BEAUTY—THE MASTER'S WAY

Did God ever say that outward beauty is wrong? I heard Chuck Swindoll give a great answer to this question one morning in a radio sermon. He said: "If the barn needs painting—paint it!" God is a really good barn painter. From the exquisite beauty of the temple to the elegance of a lily, the Scriptures give us vivid evidence of the Master's love for making things beautiful.

God cannot make anything that isn't beautiful. Everything He touches sparkles with His perfection. Outward beauty according to His design draws attention to inward beauty, and inward beauty is designed to outlive and outshine outward beauty.

> For you have been born again, not of perishable seed,
> but of imperishable, through the living and enduring
> word of God. For,
> "All men are like grass,
> and all their glory is like the flowers of the field;
> the grass withers and the flowers fall,
> but the word of the Lord stands forever."
> (1 Peter 1:23–25)

Outward beauty is intended by God to be the cover sheet for His design. Our bodies are the earthly home for our heavenly being. So go ahead—beautify your home. Paint it, dress it up, and decorate it to *His* heart's delight. But, if your heart is not beautiful, there will not be enough make-up or fine clothing to make your home a place where God will look good in you.

THE IMPOSTER'S CLOSET

The clothing found in the Impostor's closet displays the self-centeredness of his character. Those who choose to shop in his closet will find that the items inside can only be purchased at a very high cost and the fabrics from which they have been made are subject to decay.

Do you want to go shopping? Let's browse through his wardrobe and see what's all the rage in *Vanity Wear*.

- *The Fabric of Fear.* When Lorri discovered that a long lost friend was living in the same area where she would be speaking she quickly gave her a call. Lorri asked her if she would come to the event where she was scheduled to be. Her friend's voice quivered as she explained,

"No, I'm sorry, Lorri. I just have such a hard time being around groups of people even though I know most of them—it's all just too much for me. You know I've been this way all my life." Although she had been a Christian for many years, Lorri's friend was still wearing the clothes woven by the Impostor's threads of fear.

- **The Raging Colors of Anger.** Bob was a man who always wanted life to go his way or no way. One afternoon Bob discovered that a fellow worker had been given an assignment that he believed should have been given to him. At first his voice was controlled, but it was just the calm before the explosion. It began with a shout that sounded something like, "Youuuu, ooo, I just, aughhh," and then his arms started to flap up and down while he stomped his feet and kept on screaming. There wasn't much his fellow worker could say to calm him down. Bob's anger had become such a daily piece of attire that everyone who knew him walked softly while in his presence.

- **The Heavy Coat of Hostility.** While speaking in a restaurant many years ago, I noticed a man in the back of the room who seemed to be drinking in my every word. I prayed for him while I spoke, sensing he had deep needs that only Christ could fill. After the event was over, he came up to me and began spewing Bible verses in my face. He accused me of being the "whore of Babylon" and "a whitewashed sepulchre." His eyes were venomous and hateful. The manager of the restaurant quickly ushered me out of the room and called the police. I have no idea who the man was or why he reacted to my words the way that he did, but I know whose clothes he was wearing at the time.

- **The Cape of Cruelty.** Joan had lived a double life for years. At church and in her community she was known as the wife of that wonderful man who was the epitome of kindness and generosity. But at home she was the wife of an abusive husband. One evening during dinner, Joan said something that triggered her husband's temper, and he pushed his luck too far. Joan and her children left the home and gave him this ultimatum: "I love you, but I am leaving you until you get some help for your anger. When you are safe for us to live with again, we will be back." The day finally came when Steve's counselor assured Joan that her husband was ready to have his family home again. Today he is a different man. He threw his cape away and no longer rummages through the Impostor's locker looking for shrouds to cover his cruelty.

- **The Aroma of Rudeness.** I had been shopping all day with my children. At first we were having a great time, but as time wore on, I wore out. I had two coupons for pantyhose that were on sale at a store a few miles down from the mall where we were. I really wanted those pantyhose. With fifteen minutes of shopping time left, we rushed to the store. I dashed in, grabbed two pair in the right size and color and ran to the counter with three minutes to spare. The salesperson looked at me sweetly and said, "I'm sorry, but my register has just been turned off, I can't ring up any more purchases." The blood rushed to my face as I babbled, "What's the point of having a closing time if you're going to shut everything down early. I'm never going to shop here again." That was probably the nicest thing I could have said to her at that point. My children were mortified. I was also. I was never able to find that poor girl again so I could apologize for wearing the Impostor's perfume in her presence.

- **Bright Red Dress of Vulgarity.** When Alisha dropped by for a visit, Leanne fixed a hot pot of tea and sat down for a let's-get-acquainted visit. Because their husbands were both elders in their church, it just seemed right that they should know each other better. Within moments, a coarse word slipped into Alisha's sentence. Leanne was shocked but said nothing. After a while vulgar language began to flow freely from Alisha's lips until she finally said too much. Leanne could no longer stay quiet. "I'm sorry, but this kind of language is never permitted in our home. Please stop." Although Alisha came in wearing a sweatshirt and jeans, her red dress of vulgarity left a flash of lightning behind as she left.

- **The Cinched Belt of Bitterness.** During a weekend retreat, a woman tapped me on the shoulder and asked me if we could chat a while. She told me that she was particularly moved by my thoughts on forgiveness. She was a lovely woman, neatly dressed with soft red hair and a sweet smile. But her face changed as she said, "I have always been a very loving woman, and I believe that what you said about forgiving others for the wrongs they committed against us is absolutely true, but I can't and won't ever forgive my mother." We talked more about the freedom that forgiveness brings, but her spirit would not budge. Bitterness had become a restrictive piece of clothing chosen from the Impostor's closet.

- *The Running Shoes of Defeat.* Darlene grew up with a troubled soul. Her parents, though kind and loving, were pessimistic about life, and Darlene grew up with an intense need to find a purpose for her existence. She became a hippie in the 60s and an existentialist in the 70s. Having run through a variety of religions, she finally tried Christianity. But when the afterglow of her conversion dimmed, she turned to the new age movement for fulfillment. Darlene still has not found true happiness. Running after spiritual fixes in the Impostor's closet has left her empty and frustrated.

- *The Costume Jewelry of Self-Gratification.* Trudy had a habit of always running to the Impostor's closet looking for things that would make her feel good. She had a hard time saying no to herself and as a result, her credit card bills were nearly all at their limit. She decided that she needed to stay out of the shopping malls, so she found lots of projects to keep her busy at home. Then she discovered the wonder of catalogs. The TV shopping channel also brought pretty things right within the reach of her telephone. Trudy was hooked. She had visited the Impostor's storehouse so many times that she could no longer get through a day without a new look at what he had to offer. Learning to say *no* to herself and mean it has been no easy accomplishment. But she is finding that the lure of the Impostor's treasures is less seductive when she stays out of his jewelry closet.

The Impostor's closets are everywhere. No matter how hard we try we cannot cover up, paint over, or redesign the truth of the vanity that lives inside us. When it comes to the Impostor's way of inward beauty, we can't win for losing.

INWARD BEAUTY

My first trip to a publishing company was an event that I was truly looking forward to. It marked the possible beginning of a new career as a writer. Obviously, a milestone like this required a new dress. I found a great black dress on sale and decided it was perfect for the occasion. I bought it and put it in the closet. Other opportunities to wear it came and went; yet I chose to save that dress for that very special appointment.

The day finally came. I showered, put on my make-up, slipped into my new dress and looked in the mirror. It not only felt beautiful, it looked just like I hoped it would—polished, polite, and professional. I loved it. I still have that dress, and though I have worn it many times since, it has never felt *that* good again. The new feeling it had the first time I wore it is gone.

> You were taught, with regard to your former way of
> life, to put off your old self, which is being corrupted
> by its deceitful desires; to be made new in the attitude
> of your minds; and to put on the new self, created to
> be like God in true righteousness and holiness.
> (Ephesians 4:22–24)

Righteous clothing seems to always have that "first-time" feeling. Even though the garments of righteousness are hand-me-downs—having already been worn by Jesus—they are nonetheless always new. Nothing of His can grow old, become soiled, or lose its freshness. Without sin, everything remains new. Therefore, when the righteous ways of Jesus Christ become *our* ways, we make His clothing visible to the world. Each time we act like Him, we experience His life living in us. Therefore, His clothing should feel good on us. His clothing is clothing that we should long to wear. When others see us wearing His clothes we should long to hear them say, "Where did you find those garments? They're the most beautiful clothes I've ever seen." Shouldn't the beauty of the Master's clothing be more appealing to us than what can be found hanging on the Impostor's rack? A life transformed by the Master should be the best-dressed life around.

If the world's top clothing manufacturers could reproduce the Master's righteous clothing, people everywhere would want to have it and might even sell their souls to buy it. However, the fabric for Righteous-Wear is not available for mass production. Its material is invisible. You can't see it; you can only identify it by its character.

The Master has created His garments out of fabric that is crafted through the intangible effects of Jesus in us. Christianity is *Christ-in-you-ity*. His life living in you creates the pattern of the threads woven into His clothing. Holy threads wound tightly together make up a cloth so perfect, so rich in value, that only a fool would try to buy it.

As we have exposed the true value of the Impostor's clothing, let's open the doors to the Master's closet and see if we can find something more suitable to wear by seeing pictures of how it looks on others.

- *The Fresh New Look of Love.* The night we brought our daughter home from the hospital was a very special evening. In those ancient times, fathers weren't allowed to touch their babies until they left the hospital so by the time Bud held Annette in his arms, she was already seven days old. Late that evening, I sat in bed and watched him rocking our crying child to sleep in his arms. There was a look on his face that I have only seen three times. The first time was when he watched me walk down the aisle to become his wife, and the other two were reserved for his first real look at his babies. Though he often wears loving expressions on his face, these three events were different; they were moments when Bud was surprised by love. I believe every act of kindness, every forgiving word, every happy time shared with my husband is somehow still connected to those moments when the look in his eyes said, "I didn't know I'd love you so much."

- *The Forgiven Look of Joy*. When Lawrence stood in front of our congregation at Grace Community Church, his face lit up the auditorium. As the father of one of our pastors and the husband of a godly woman, Lawrence had the gospel living all around him. Then the day came when he was asked a personal question, "Lawrence, how about you? Do you know where you are going when you die?" That afternoon Lawrence gave his heart to Jesus. When Pastor Dennis brought Lawrence up to share the news the following Sunday, both heaven and earth joined in the applause. A few weeks later Lawrence's son Larry had the joy of baptizing his father. Lawrence wears the look of joy that flows from a forgiven heart.
- *The Soft Cover of Peace*. Ellen loved God with all her

being. She was one of the most peaceful women I have ever known. As the mother of four children, Ellen had many opportunities to be fussed up by her children. Yet, each time I watched her courteous manner while handling their disputes, I wondered what it would take to shake her tranquility. Then Ellen's son was killed in a car accident. When I visited my friend I expected to find her shattered and discouraged. Instead, Ellen greeted me at the door with a pleasant smile on her face. She held out her arms to comfort *me*. When I asked her how she was handling her loss, she said, "I just cry with God and with my husband. I know where my son is now, and I can't wait to hold him again in heaven. But till then, I am thankful for the pleasure he has been to us, and I am so grateful that God considered us worthy of raising him for this very short time." Now, twenty years later, she still wears the soft covering of peace that has kept her warm to the Spirit of God through all the circumstances of her life.

- *Strong Fabric of Patience.* For the first time ever, Mandy made it through a whole church service without a wiggle or an outbreak of tears. Mandy had a severe problem with Attention Deficit Disorder. She required consistent love and discipline. Her mother, who was her homeschool teacher, seldom missed a beat when it came to combining firm instruction with kind application. Many moms would have caved in after a few weeks of trying to subdue her child's erratic mood swings, but Mandy's mother maintained a cool temper. Many mothers would have felt embarrassed by her behavior, but Mandy's mother openly praised every time her daughter showed success in self-control. The fabric of Mandy's mom is woven together with strong threads of good character that don't tear when stretched to the limit.

- *Cape of Kindness.* I stood at the back of the banquet hall watching the women parade through the room to find their places at their tables. I had come to the conference to manage the bookstore; therefore, it wouldn't have been appropriate for me to join the women during the luncheon. I felt like a hungry child with her nose pressed against the window of a bakery. Then Alice spotted me from across the room. She quickly jumped up and hurried over to me and said, "Sandy, I have an extra seat at my table, you must come and join us, I don't want you to miss hearing the speaker." As Alice took off her cape of kindness and wrapped it around me, my feelings of not belonging melted away. Her act of compassion is nothing new; it's just the way Alice is.

- *Sweet Aroma of Gentleness.* Pastor Edwards is a man of truly gentle character. Though a tower of strength in his convictions, his quiet manner makes even his words of correction acceptable. He was the first person who was brave enough to share the gospel with my husband. He was the one who encouraged me to love Bud through the worst times in our marriage. And it was he who performed the celebration of the renewal of our wedding vows. Pastor Edwards holds a place in my heart as one of the most beautiful servants of God I have ever known. The fragrance of his gentleness will follow Bud and me into every anniversary we share.

- *Veil of Goodness.* Norma McCorvey was used to being used. Men used her and then tossed her aside when they got tired of her. The feminists used her to be their poster woman in the trial of Roe vs. Wade. Even the pro-life community used her as their symbol of the evils of the court decision that made abortion on demand legal. It took the love of a little girl whose heart was without guile to love Norma to Jesus. When I interviewed Norma and her young evangelist one afternoon, I felt as if I were speaking to two children, one who had never known the corruptive effects of sin and the other who had been cleansed of it. Purity gave birth to purity when a seven-year-old girl covered a tired woman with the Master's veil of goodness.

- *The Walking Shoes of Faithfulness.* Iris had been a loving wife and mother. She worked tirelessly in her home and she served her family well. Then Iris began to show the beginning stages of a mysterious illness. A falter in her steps, a slur of her words eventually led to many trips to the doctor. She was soon diagnosed with multiple sclerosis. For the last two decades of her life, Iris's husband daily said good-bye to the wife he once knew and became instead her caretaker. With never a word of complaint, her husband faithfully stayed by her side, ministering to her needs with enduring love and compassion. His faith was tested and proven, as he loved her through the last days of her life. Today he continues to wear the walking shoes of faith as he travels alone with the God who carried them through the fire.

- *The Shining Stones of Self-Control.* The Book of Proverbs tells us that a woman of noble character is more valuable than precious costly stones. I met a young woman many years ago who was engaged to be married. She was so in love with her husband-to-be that she wanted to give him a special gift on their wedding night. She had battled a weight problem most of her life, and she wanted to conquer the problem before she said, "I do." So she found a healthy diet and committed herself to stick to it up to the day that she put on her wedding gown. I watched her as she was transformed into a radiant bride all prepared to give herself to her husband as a beautiful gift. Today she is the same size as she was a decade ago. She doesn't fret over her weight, she just allows her eating habits to reflect her desire to always be the best she can be for the man she married. Her self-control has rewarded her with more than a lovely body. She has become a woman of noble character as she has been shaped by her consistent choice to say *no* to herself and *yes* to her God in all the many areas of her life.

THE MASTER'S PLAN FOR BEAUTY

The evidence that we are wearing the Master's clothing is seen through the ways we wear His life in us. These ways are manifested through hands that lift and serve the weary, feet that walk away from evil, and lips that spread His blessings everywhere. His clothing sparkles with a kind of radiance that spreads joy across the faces of those who thought life was hopeless. Righteous clothing is seen through righteous deeds that spring from righteous character. It is the result of right living.

His righteous clothing is what we wear on the inside. The only way to obtain it is to receive it through the One who purchased it for us two thousand years ago on a cross on a hill called Calvary.

The purpose of God's beauty is to define our identity. Outward beauty defines what we are, and inward beauty defines Whose we are.

> Therefore, as God's chosen people, holy and dearly loved, clothe yourselves with compassion, kindness, humility, gentleness and patience. Bear with each other and forgive whatever grievances you may have against one another. Forgive as the Lord forgave you. And over all these virtues put on love, which binds them all together in perfect unity.
>
> Let the peace of Christ rule in your hearts, since as members of one body you were called to peace. And be thankful. Let the word of Christ dwell in you richly as you teach and admonish one another with all wisdom, and as you sing psalms, hymns and spiritual songs with gratitude in your hearts to God. And whatever you do, whether in word or deed, do it all in the name of the Lord Jesus, giving thanks to God the Father through him. (Colossians 3:12–17)

After God created Adam, He gave him the responsibility of giving names to all the animals. While Adam worked, he saw that each of God's creatures had mates who had the same distinctive qualities that made them a match. Then he looked at himself and realized he was alone. He couldn't find one creature that looked like him. Then God made Eve. Adam took one look at her and exclaimed, "Wow, ah-ha, this is it!" Or as the Scripture says,

"This is now bone of my bones,
And flesh of my flesh;
She shall be called Woman,
Because she was taken out of Man."
(Genesis 2:23, NASB)

At last Adam had someone with whom he could relate, thus he named her woman because he clearly saw that she came from him and was a part of him—she was a perfect match. Her beauty on the outside told Adam that she, like him, was a human being, different from all the other creatures in the Garden. Her inward beauty identified her as created in the image of their Creator. Like Adam, she was perfect and holy, possessing the character of the God who made them.

Then at the terrible point in the story when Eve succumbed to the serpent, Eve became unlike her husband and God. She was now alone. Although her outward appearance defined her as human, her inward being defied both her beauty and her identity. Then Adam followed suit and bit the fruit. The Impostor had succeeded in his plan to confuse their identity so that they would not recognize the beauty marks of the Master, and they would lose their right to wear His clothing.

But the Master was unwilling to give up on His created children. The cross of Christ was in His heart even at the time of the Fall. The cross has opened the door for us to come back to the Master. When we see the beauty of His heart, the glory of His character shines on us and makes us beautiful in Him. His kind of beauty improves with age until during our last moments on earth we can sing the words that flowed so easily from the lips of the old woman who whispered softly in my ear, "Jesus, Jesus, oh, how I love Him."

> He has made everything beautiful in its time. He has
> also set eternity in the hearts of [women].
> (Ecclesiastes 3:11a)

EPILOGUE TO BEAUTY

Rising early aboard the *Sensuous Sea*, the picture of beauty in its purest form often greets our senses with perfect delight. The water clear as glass, a fresh smell of sea air, the quiet chirping of birds waking the dawn, lift my thoughts toward heaven. There is no other place to deliver my praise but to the Creator who shares my joy for the whole glorious event. No wonder even the hardest of souls is often convinced of omnipotence when confronted with such unexplainable beauty. To whom else can we turn when life spits ugly on us? We turn to the Beautiful One.

Do you feel surly today? Need a makeover? Have you always dreamed of being the beautiful swan but feel instead like the ugly duckling? Why go to the closet of the fashion designer who peddles soiled goods? Turn to the Master, and let Him clothe you with the beauty that showered light across the manger and splashed crimson on the ground beneath the cross. Turn your gaze toward the heavens where He colored the sky with such brilliance that men could hardly bear to watch Him as He disappeared into the clouds. His beauty awaits you. It is the beauty that when seen by others causes them to say, "Ah-ha, so this is what God is like."

The Call of the Imposter

Oh, how serious you are about something that is meant to be light and pleasurable. Beauty is only skin deep, after all, so why be in such a downer over it? Have some flair, have some style, and have some beauty on me.

Haven't you seen the new colors for this year? They're you! Go get them, it will make you feel better. In fact, that is what beauty is all about; it makes you feel so much better about yourself, your circumstances, and your life.

Your answers to life are inside of you. Reach down, dig deep, and you will see what I mean. You're wonderful. You have a oneness of spirituality that has been a part of the universe since the beginning of time.

There is no real joy in being unattractive. But look at the ones who would tell you that you must learn to sacrifice yourself and become a loathsome servant in order to feel beautiful. Such hypocrisy. Do they look beautiful to you? Those faces of martyrdom, those expressions of self-righteousness; it's perfectly nauseating. Now stop envying what you don't need and start reaching for what you do need. Time is clicking by, and if you really want to be beautiful you're going to have to begin right now.

I am here to help you know what looks good on you and what doesn't. Let me be your personal shopper and together we can transform your life in ways you could never have imagined. So, are you ready? Let's go shopping.

The Call of the Master

Who can define beauty for you? My enemy makes light of the subject because his soul is too vile to comprehend the splendor of it. He cannot create beauty; therefore, he is unable to reproduce it according to My design. He is a fraud who sells his imitations of the real thing to people who have not known the truth.

But you know the truth. There is only one way for beauty to be corrupted, and that way is through sin. I have washed you clean from sin's stains, I have wrapped you in My righteous clothing, and I see you through My Son who is perfect in My eyes.

My garments have been custom-made for you. I have watched the way you wear them. Your righteous deeds have not escaped My attention. I have seen how tenderly you touch those who are discouraged and downhearted. I have enjoyed the wisdom that fills your thoughts as you spend time in My Word. Your love for your family and your friends blesses My heart more than you can know. Yes, My child, you are beautiful today, and you will be more beautiful tomorrow. The older you are the more stunning you become. All heaven breathes in your exquisite elegance.

I am looking forward to the time when My work will be accomplished and you will be the radiant bride I have created you to be. Till then trust Me and know that everything I touch turns beautiful.

The Heart of
Friendship

A friend will mold a heroine
out of a common woman.

<small>BARBARA JENKINS, WIT AND WISDOM FOR WOMEN</small>

CHAPTER NINE

It happens all the time. While browsing quietly through the greeting cards in your local gift shop, a wacky woman jabs you with her elbow and shoves a card into your face. *"Did you see this one? Here read it, it's great!"* I confess—I am that woman. I'm a funny card nut. The good ones are written to be shared; isn't that why we call them *greeting cards?* Here are three of my all-time favorites.

One: A beautiful, well-groomed spaniel is pertly pictured on the front of the card. The scene looks more like a fine painting than a photograph. With an air of pompousness the dog says, "I made you a present for your birthday." Then when you open the card, he explains, "It's in the backyard."

Two: The drawing on the front of the card is of a woman in a business suit with a cup of Java hanging from her index finger. Her cartooned expression illustrates a lack of sincerity as she muses, "Heard you were sick." On the inside the greeting continues, "Hope you don't die."

Three: A drawing of a beatnik greets you on the front of the card. He's wearing a beret, has a goatee, and he's holding an espresso in his hand. With a look of boredom on his face he sings; "Happy birthday to you, Happy birthday to you, Happy birthday to you..." A peak inside and his true self is revealed, "It's always about you, isn't it?"

You can see why other shoppers find me so resistible.

There are, however, some valuable points to be made from the sarcasm of those flippant greetings. We all need friends. But, the kind of friends we need are the ones who will give us their best, earnestly care about how we are, and love us with selfless affection.

TAKING THE NEED TEST

Friends come to us in many makes and models. Some are fair-weathered, flitting into our lives for a season, and some end up staying a lifetime. Some make your life a party, some a picnic, and some just make you want to leave town and change your name.

One of the Impostor's strategies of war with the Master is to either isolate us away from the friends who will make a meaningful difference in our lives or to encircle us with friends who will broadside us on our road to spiritual maturity.

Maybe you are one who doesn't particularly feel the need for friends. Or possibly, you are at a stage in life where you just don't have much time for them. Perhaps your heart still bears the bruises from a person you trusted to be your friend. No matter how you might feel about friendship, we all need friends. Let me encourage you to take the following test to help you identify the unique place that friendship needs to have in our lives.

The Need Test
- Something wonderful has happened to you; who is the first person you think of telling?
- Someone you care about has just broken your trust; whom do you need to be near?

- You have some free time and you want to play; who is your playmate?
- You are afraid; whom do you call?
- You are lonely; whom do you miss?
- You are troubled and need counsel; to whom do you turn?
- You are discouraged and ready to quit; to whom do you reach out?
- You are impassioned by great vision; with whom do you lock arms?
- You need prayer support; in whom do you confide?
- You are under attack; in whom do you hide?

We may have a tendency to say that God meets all of those needs. And certainly He does. And if we are married, our husband's name usually goes on the list. But that is not a complete answer. Because no one person can possibly meet all of our many and complicated needs, God directs a variety of people to come into our lives to grow us, stretch us, and shape us into a congregation of people whom He has chosen to be His earth-links to heaven.

The Master has created a planet of people and has plunked us smack dab in the middle of them so that we can affect each other's lives for His good and for His glory. When that takes place friendship happens. Extending and receiving God's love to and through others is what friendship is all about.

Five Friends and a King

David was the youngest of eight sons and his home was bursting at the seams with boyish pranks, and man-sized appetites. Though David was often given to long periods of solitude, he was also a man who was accustomed to being around people. Throughout the course of David's life he was surrounded by many friends. Some of his friends were better to him than brothers, and some abused his trust through acts of scandalous betrayal.

First, there was Jonathan, the perfect friend. As the son of King Saul, Jonathan was next in line to become Israel's king. Yet, Jonathan often risked his own life to protect his friend from his father's murderous intentions. He died knowing that the crown would be appointed to the friend whom he had loved with selfless loyalty. Jonathan's zeal for God and his affection for his friend superceded any claim to fame that he could possibly have had.

> He who loves a pure heart and whose speech is gracious will have the king for his friend. (Proverbs 22:11)

Next, there was Joab—a man of extreme contradictions. He was a man of God, a man of violence, a man of loyalty, and a man of treason. As the captain of King David's army, he had close access to David. Though he often displayed great loyalty to the king, his treasonous actions in the end proved that he was the kind of friend who used the power of others for his own personal gain. As most men of bloodshed do, Joab died by the sword.

> The kisses of an enemy may be profuse, but faithful are the wounds of a friend. (Proverbs 27:6)

Then, we find Nathan. His words cut like a knife, yet they anointed David's conscience with the healing balm of truth. As a prophet in the king's court, Nathan knew the sins that David committed. David had become an adulterer and a murderer. His kingdom was crumbling around him, and his body was being eaten away by guilt. Nathan confronted his friend knowing that the king had the authority to have him put to death if he didn't like the way the conversation went. Nathan's faithful obedience to God and his tender compassion for his friend compelled him to speak the truth. David was broken before God because of his sin. He repented for the crimes he had committed and through God's mercy his throne was restored to him. God used the council of a friend to save the kingdom.

> My dear friends, if you know people who have wandered off from God's truth, don't write them off. Go after them. Get them back and you will have rescued precious lives from destruction and prevented an epidemic of wandering away from God. (James 5:19–20, *The Message*)

Last, we have Ahithophel and Hushai the fourth and fifth examples of friendship in the life of David. These two men were counselors to the king. One was fickle—the other was faithful. When David's own son Absalom began a campaign to unseat his father from the throne, he sought to enlist the support of his father's best people. Ahithophel took a look at David, who was showing the wear and tear of age, then turned to Absalom, full of youthful vigor, and became the counter-intelligence agent for Absalom's death squad. Hushai saw the recklessness of Absalom's youth and the wisdom of David's years in office and brought a halt to Ahithophel's subversion by launching a counterattack on his counsel. Once again, God intervened to spare the King through the courage of a faithful friend.

> Even my close friend, whom I trusted, he who shared my bread, has lifted up his heel against me. (Psalm 41:9)

> Perfume and incense bring joy to the heart, and the pleasantness of one's friend springs from his earnest counsel. (Proverbs 27:9)

THE MASTERS' GRACIOUS GARDEN OF FRIENDS

It's easy for outgoing people to preach sermons to everyone else about the need for friends. I am a woman who loves people; lots of people. When I walk into a room, I whisper to myself, "This is my place and these are my people." My fingers itch with the urge to touch every single one of them.

Nevertheless, as we have seen in the life of another people person, having lots of friends can often leave you more vulnerable to disloyalty than living safely with just a few carefully selected companions.

As I review the many people who have been active participants in my life, I find that none of them have appeared by accident. Instead, each one was perfectly planted by the hand of the Master. Built within the framework of His design, He has called certain people to come alongside me to grow me, shape me, inspire me, instruct me, and even to let me be wounded so that I could become more like Him.

My dear friend Diana tops the list as the friend whom I have known the longest. We met in third grade. We became sisters when we picked our scabs (we were too squeamish to prick our fingers) and joined our blood together. Then we each cut off a piece of our hair and buried it on the corner where we lived. Now as grown women, we still treasure that special bond that has endured throughout the years and feels as comfortable as an old pair of slippers.

Diana lives in California and I live in Oregon. We have been there for each other despite the miles between us. Last year when my mother died, Diana and her husband, Darrell, came to Mom's funeral to share our grief. A few days after the service, we stayed with them in their home and spent several hours reminiscing about two girls whose childhoods had so much in common. Now we have both been orphaned—each having said good-bye to our parents. The last time Diana visited me in my home, we spent our three days going through all our photographs of her and me together. We made them into memory albums that trace the history of our friendship. Diana gives me roots. We are indeed fortunate if we have a friend who can touch our hand and say, "I knew you when…"

I met Gladys shortly after I rededicated my life to Christ. As young believers in a new church we became fast friends. In those early years I knew absolutely nothing about the Bible. Gladys patiently listened to me as I talked on and on about the things I was learning and discovering in God's Word. One day, Gladys made a startling comment to me that inspired my heart for ministry. She said, "Sandy, someday God is going to use you to teach other women from His word." A few years later, as I was driving through our neighborhood, God confirmed her words by pressing on my heart a deep burden for the needs of women and a desire to serve them through the teaching of His Word. Gladys awakened my heart to vision because she spoke the heart of the Master to me. We all need a friend who will show us our place in God's kingdom.

Alvina was a pint-sized bundle of energy. The wife of a pastor, Alvina was the first older woman in my life who showed me how to love my husband and children and to make my home a wonderful place to be. I jogged across the street often so I could sit at her table and listen to her as she told me stories about her life and her family. When she talked about God's faithfulness to her in all her life's circumstances, she made God real to me. On every visit, she would bring out her china teacups and a plate of fresh baked goodies. I do that today when my friends come to visit me. (Though I prefer mugs—they're bigger!) Alvina always made me feel like I was the most important part of her day. We all need a woman friend who will model for us what a godly wife and mother looks like.

Alvina and I also became comrades in Christ. Shortly after moving into our new home, we began a Bible study with our neighbors. Her example of optimistic love for those women inspired me to follow her example. All that I do in service to others had its early beginnings in Alvina's motherly love. She gave me tools for maturity. We all need a friend who will mentor us so that we will know how to mentor others.

With her tiny voice and quiet spirit, Carol has shown me how to see myself from the Master's perspective. Carol chooses to see others through the eyes of mercy. Having experienced the unconditional love of God in her own life, she is quick to love others. The afternoon Carol and I met, we each shared how we had come to know Christ as our Savior. I learned that Carol had accepted Christ on her deathbed. She had, just a few years earlier, been admitted into the hospital with heart failure, kidney failure, pneumonia, and strep throat. Carol became Oregon's first kidney transplant recipient, but it was her new heart in Christ that gave her a life transplant. Our hearts were knitted together that afternoon.

Carol came into my life at a time when I could only see how much I was lacking in my walk with Christ. She always saw the amazing things that God was doing in me. Comments like, "Oh, Sandy, it hurts me when you put yourself down so much." And, "I am always so amazed by the ways that God has gifted you. You are so special to me," kept me going when I felt like quitting. Carol's sweet spirit is a fresh aroma of God's affirming love for me. Everyone needs a friend who sees us through God's eyes.

I saw Mona from across the church and something inside of me told me that she and I needed to become friends. The only problem with my good intentions to become her friend was that Mona couldn't stand me. Though she accepted my many invitations to lunch and allowed me to sit with her at Bible studies, the look in her eyes seemed to say, "Could you just go away now?" But I was not about to give up that easily. For two years, I continued to cultivate a friendship with Mona. There were moments when it would seem that she was warming up to me, but then the next time I saw her, she would flash that, "Can't you just go somewhere else?" look at me. Then one day while we were stuck in a car together for a five-hour trip, Mona made a shocking confession. She said,

"Sandy, you have probably noticed that I haven't exactly enjoyed being around you." It was all I could do to keep from saying something obvious like, "Well, duh!" But I bit my tongue and let her direct the conversation. "The reason why I haven't liked you is because I've hated your joy. I'm so sorry for the ways I've treated you. I really want what you have." Mona's words affirmed to me that God loves to bring the friends of *His* choosing into our lives. Everyone needs a friend who will let you be a friend to them.

My sister, Rosanne, who knew Christ long before I did, has become to me more than a sister. She inspires me with her nonstop energy and her ability to be a servant to all those with whom she comes in contact. Our friendship grew as we became adult women with a common need to put our difficult childhood into perspective with God's sovereign plan for our lives.

Throughout the years, my sister has raised six children and helped her husband achieve his calling to become a minister and subsequently a chaplain in the army. Rosanne now serves with her husband by coming alongside the military wives, helping them to adjust to the demands of their husband's careers, and showing them how to live fruitful lives for Christ. She continues to stay close to her married kids and keeps up with her growing number of grandchildren. The word *can't* doesn't exist in her vocabulary.

Today Rosanne is one of my strongest sources of encouragement. Always believing that her sister can do anything, she sings my praises everywhere she goes. Everyone needs a friend who is also a cheerleader.

Grace is everyone's friend. She is one of those women who teaches younger women how to grow old. She has been at death's door many times during the last few years—just when we think she is going home to heaven she bounces back to life again. Wherever she is, whether in a hospital bed or a Bible study, Grace faithfully shares the wonderful love of Jesus with everyone she sees. She is bright and cheerful no matter how she feels, and she never wastes her time in conversations that aren't reflective of the love of God. As her faith grows stronger than her body, she is a living example of how to live for Christ with every second you have. Everyone needs a friend who can show them how to grow old gracefully.

Others are friends who believe that I can do whatever God calls me to do. Connie, Susan, Alice, and Bunny are four who have not only encouraged me to write this book but each one has, in her own special way, put forth time and energy to help me to see the project through to completion. Connie came and picked up my ironing one day when it was dividing and multiplying in the laundry room. Susan helped me get promotional materials ready to send to the publishing companies. Alice met with me often to give me editorial input regarding each chapter. And Bunny not only read my work but also kept me mindful of God's call on my life to write it. Everyone needs friends who will be God's voice, hands, and feet when work needs to be done.

Some friends are wonderful playmates and workmates who make my life fun and follow along with me on great adventures. Sandy, for example, can always be counted on to tackle any task that is too big for one person to handle. Bud and I were in the process of remodeling our kitchen just before my mother-in-law came home to live with us. I had only one day to get the kitchen painted before Mom arrived. Because she was terminally ill, I knew the smell of paint would make her uncomfortable. Sandy came to the door with her paint roller in hand, and in a few hours the job was done to perfection. On Wednesday nights you will find us with our easels and oil paints encouraging each other to become better artists with Stan our expert teacher. Sandy makes work and play a pleasure. Everyone needs friends who will keep joy and laughter in our lives as we accomplish the tasks that are before us.

There are visionaries who love new challenges and have invincible courage to dream great things for God. They are the ones who inspire new ministries and add polish to existing ones. Women with deep wisdom keep my feet on a steady course of spiritual growth by sharing their joys and struggles as they follow the Master's plan for their lives. Prayer warriors see the impossibilities in my life as possibilities when brought before the Master's throne. I belong to two special prayer groups who take my requests seriously and can be counted on to uphold me when the circumstances in my life are too heavy to be carried alone. Everyone needs friends who will keep the flame of faith alive and growing as we serve in the Master's kingdom.

What a privilege it is to be so loved by God's children. Each one adds something wonderful to my life. I am who I am today because of the people that God has strategically called to come alongside me. I see God in them, and I see God in me because of them.

But not all have been bundles of blessings. When you allow many people in your life, you can't help but be wounded by a few of them from time to time. There have been some that left me stranded during times of crisis. A few were fickle-hearted and pushed me aside for other more attractive friends. Some betrayed my trust.

The painful episodes that I have experienced in friendship are not unique. Most of us get hurt while seeking to build what we hope will become lasting friendships in the Master's family. I have experienced the temptation of wanting to shut the door to my heart so that no one can come in to hurt me again. But I have also learned that to retreat because we've been mistreated in the process of making friends is exactly what the Impostor hopes we will do. If we turn away from friendship, we won't discover the other side of the story.

Being wounded by people who were supposed to be your friends is not a one-way street. Through the pain that I have experienced, I have seen more clearly how I have hurt others also. I believe that God has allowed each painful moment, each feeling of abandonment, each breach of trust, each broken promise to show me what kind of a friend I have been to others.

Who called these hurtful women to come into my life? I am sure that when the offenses were first inflicted the Impostor thought that they would beat me into defeat. Instead, the Master has used each one to add strength, maturity, and wisdom to my growth as His daughter. Through all the ups and downs in friendship I have learned and am learning still how wonderful it feels to forgive, how able God is to meet my needs during the worst of times, and how to love my friends the way God loves me.

God never shuts the door of His heart to us. Instead, He flings it open and says:

Come in.
I know you will hurt Me
but come in.

I know you will misunderstand Me,
but come in.
I know you will run off and forget that I am here for you—
but nevertheless, come in.
Come in because I have something wonderful for you.
Come in and find how much I love you.
Come in and see how I see you.
Just come in.
Don't worry about how you look or what you've done
or how unholy you feel right now
Just come in
My heart is waiting to be your friend.

SANDY SNAVELY 1999

All of my friends are more than acquaintances to me; they are the evidence of God's heart for friendship.

THE MASTER'S PURPOSE AND PRINCIPLES FOR FRIENDSHIP

Friendship was born in the heart of the Master. He had friends. Abraham, Moses, and David were among just a few of those whom He called friends. Jesus also had friends. Though He deeply loved all of His disciples, Peter, James, and John were counted among His special friends, as were Mary, Martha, and Lazarus. And Jesus said that we are His friends if we do what He has commanded.

You and I are the friends of the Master. When we come into His heart and see His heart of friendship waiting for us we will come away with a perfect pattern for how we can build friendships with others. When I observe the way of His friendship toward us, I find again that He has given me a pattern for how I am to be a friend to others.

His way of friendship can be found wherever the descriptions of love are written in the Word of God and can be tied together with Jesus' summation of the law. First, we are to love God with *all* our heart, *all* our mind, and with *all* our strength. And second, we are to love our neighbors as ourselves. This command sets the basis for *all* of our earthly relationships. All we need to know about how to express the love of God to others is contained in the power of these words.

Remember the caption on the third greeting card in the beginning of this chapter: "It's always about you, isn't it?" Friendship, the Master's way, is not *always* about us. Though He uses friendship to grow us, stretch us, shape us, mold us, inspire us, and even wound us, friendship is not only for our own growth and amusement. Friendship teaches us how to be to others what God has been to us. We have the opportunity, through friendship, to do what a child once said to his mother after a friend had hurt him, "I know God is there, Mommy, but I need to be hugged by Jesus with skin on." We are the physical "skin on" reproductions of God's love for others.

Friendship according to the Master's design takes time, work, and perseverance. It begins by having the Master's heart for the purpose of friendship and submitting to His plan no matter what the personal costs may be. We may need to open or reopen the doors of our lives to let other people come in to the inner places where we live. Knowing that we may be hurt again is not a good enough reason to keep the door locked and shut.

I am seldom a person that is given to giving in. When life kicks me I usually kick it back. It's a family thing. But while serving in the church where I was a member, a division erupted between two women's ministry groups. One group was an evening program that was geared to meet the women's needs for fun and fellowship. The other was the daytime Bible study designed to challenge women to grow spiritually. I was the coordinator of the daytime Bible study. To this day I don't know how the conflict got started, but I remember vividly what it looked and felt like.

Some of the women who were actively involved in the two groups began to sneer as they passed each other in the hall on Sunday mornings. Members of each group defended the importance of *their* work above what the other was doing. Some women felt disloyal while attending the *other* group's programs, so they stayed away from them. Because of the position I held as the Bible study leader, I was sometimes a target for rumors. One day I discovered a rumor had been circulating that I had told women that our group was more *spiritual* than the other. When I tried to clear up the misunderstanding I was misunderstood. Being a women's ministry leader hurt.

For years after that painful experience, I was terrified to walk back into anything that looked like an organized women's program. I pushed aside the burden that God had placed on my heart for women and found other ways to serve the body of Christ. I taught Sunday school, I spoke to women in other churches, and I ministered to the body of Christ while doing my talk show. But my heart still longed to get back to where I knew God wanted me to be. Finally the day came when I was asked to teach a women's Bible study at our new church. I was terrified, but I knew it was time to say yes to God, to fling wide the doors, and to let our women come in. Today my heart is more passionate about the needs of women than it has ever been before. I am tougher than I was before. Hurt doesn't hurt me the way it used to. I have found that ministry isn't all about me, it's about walking hand in hand with the Master on behalf of His people.

God made us for Him and for each other.

Betrayed, hurt, and abandoned, Jesus gave Himself to us as our friend. His example is ours to follow. He never picked up His marbles and ran home when the game failed to make Him a winner. Love compelled Him to endure the pain of loving us, knowing that we were helpless to learn how to love others without Him. Knowing we would turn our backs on Him, ignore Him, misunderstand Him, use Him for our own gain, choose other friends to worship, and be too embarrassed to call Him our friend when in the company of His enemies, were among the very reasons He chose to be our friend. His response to our inability to comprehend His offer of flawless friendship is our pattern for developing friendships that He can be proud of.

Just like walking, talking, and learning to eat with a spoon, friendship is something that is taught. There are ways to build strong, productive, enduring friendships and there are ways to kill our friendships. There's no better time than now to fling wide the gates of our hearts and let the people come in. But, before we do that, let's read the directions on how to tear down a friend and how to build one.

HOW TO TEAR DOWN A FRIEND

- Live a worldly life; ignore the Holy Spirit's renewal process for you.
- Refuse to acknowledge or to be a part of God's kingdom plan for your life.

- Cling to your friend—be possessive of her time, affection, and loyalty, and smother her with your need for her attention.
- Judge your friend when she strays from the truth, and don't encourage her to return to the Master's heart.
- When she is hurting, struggling, or in need of protection, run the other way.
- Be jealous of your friend's position, gifts, talents, and do all you can to keep her from reaching her God-given potential.
- Encourage your friend to ignore the God-ordained priorities in her life. Interfere with and interrupt the time she needs to spend with her family.
- Teach your friend by example how to live a mediocre life in Christ.
- When your friend appears to be going down in defeat, go with those who are more successful.
- Destroy your friend's reputation by slandering her behind her back.
- Don't pray for her.
- Don't forgive her.

HOW TO BUILD A FRIEND

- Let God be the one to choose your friends.
- Let your love for Christ be the foundation and cornerstone of your friendships.
- Be the new person that God has created you to be.
- Keep God's purpose and direction as the main focus for your life.
- Love your friend with your hands empty, expecting no return on your investment of love and loyalty.

- Sacrifice time, pain, and reputation to uphold and support your friend when her circumstances are grim.
- Encourage your friend to be faithful to God's ordained priorities for her life. Set her free to serve her family without your interference or interruptions.
- Keep reminding her and challenging her to pursue God's plan for her life at the risk of personal loss. Let her go if God leads her away from you.
- Risk speaking the truth in love when your friend shows signs of weakening in her walk with Christ.
- Encourage your friend to have other best friends.
- Be your friend's constant cheerleader.
- Pray for your friend.
- Forgive your friend.

LEARNING TO BE A GOD SPOTTER FOR OUR FRIENDS

Most everything I know about being a Christian I have learned from someone else. Gerry Breshears, a professor of theology and a good friend who is an elder at my church, preached a sermon recently that took the subject of friendship from black and white and put it into living color. He used a phrase that clarified what friendship looks like. He called it "being a God spotter for someone else."

A God spotter is the person we need to have near us when life pushes us off balance, when plans don't go our way, when solutions are lost in the circumstances of our problems, when we throw up our hands and shout, "Where is God in all this mess?" The God spotter comes in and says, "Oh, look, there He is!"

The friends I've introduced you to have been wonderful

God spotters in my life. They have found Him in the places where I had failed to look. God spotters are sprinkled throughout the kingdom of God. Some of them are our friends and family. Some minister to us in our churches through the preaching and teaching of the Word. Some are people with whom we share letters and long-distance phone calls. And some have passed on to heaven, but the results of their God spotting remains with us.

A good God spotter is someone who knows God intimately and is able to identify His character, His actions, and His will in their lives and in the lives of others. God spotters believe that all the affairs of our lives matter to God. They also know His Word. It's hard to spot God if you don't know what He looks like or where to find Him.

But how can you spot a God spotter? They will be the ones who can say to you:

- When disaster looks like abandonment—
  "Have I not commanded you? Be strong and courageous. Do not be terrified; do not be discouraged, for the LORD your God will be with you wherever you go" (Joshua 1:9).
- When loneliness consumes you—
  "Here I am! I stand at the door and knock. If anyone hears my voice and opens the door, I will come in and eat with him, and he with me" Revelation (3:20).
- When you're angry with others—
  "Bear with each other and forgive whatever grievances you may have against one another. Forgive as the Lord forgave you" (Colossians 3:13).
- When you don't know which way to turn—

"Let us then approach the throne of grace with confidence, so that we may receive mercy and find grace to help us in our time of need" (Hebrews 4:16).

- When you wonder if your faith is real—
"Fight the good fight of the faith. Take hold of the eternal life to which you were called when you made your good confession in the presence of many witnesses" (1 Timothy 6:12).

- When you are tempted by the Impostor's lies—
"Be self-controlled and alert. Your enemy the devil prowls around like a roaring lion looking for someone to devour. Resist him, standing firm in the faith, because you know that your brothers throughout the world are undergoing the same kind of sufferings" (1 Peter 5:8–9).

- When you feel like giving up—
"Be faithful, even to the point of death, and I will give you the crown of life" (Revelation 2:10b).

The Impostor will do all he can to keep us from having God spotters in our lives. He hates our friendships when they are patterned according to the Master's plan. If he can lure us away from the need of friends, from being a Christlike example of friendship, and from rising above the hurts that friends can sometimes inflict, he will have us right where he wants us— in the palm of the world's hand.

In the world, friendship has no purpose other than to satisfy the needs of the individual first. It has no plan, so it makes up the rules as it goes along. It has no example to follow, so it imitates what might look like the real thing. As the Impostor strives to destroy the kingdom of the Master, he sends his emissaries on a mission to divide, isolate, and devour the people of God. Fearing the little power that is ours when we are by ourselves, he is terrified of the thunder that erupts when we are together.

I, for one, am more than happy to struggle through the difficulties of being a people person just to see the Impostor lose the battle within the sphere of friends appointed to me by the Master. If there is blood to be spilled on the battlefield of our flesh, I want the DNA to match the servants of the Impostor who failed to conquer the fortresses built by the Master's friends.

> *A mighty fortress is our God,*
> *A bulwark never failing;*
> *Our helper He, amidst the flood*
> *Of mortal ills prevailing.*
> *For still our ancient foe*
> *Does seek to work us woe;*
> *His craft and power are great,*
> *And armed with cruel hate,*
> *On earth is not His equal.*

MARTIN LUTHER

The Call of the Impostor

Actually, it really is all about you. If you keep listening to those who think they are wise, you will exhaust yourself and waste your energies on useless pursuits for unnecessary causes.

Friendship is the garden you plant when you want to see and smell flowers. But make no mistake of it; you are the gardener. The trowel is in your hands. You can plant whatever you wish and uproot whatever causes you pain. Fences make good neighbors, so build your fence as tall as you need to so that your garden will be well protected.

Choose your friends wisely. End your friendships just as wisely. Forgiveness is for fools who love to be hurt. Dignity comes when you can rise above the carnal need for kinship and freely select the people with whom you have something in common. When there is no longer support for each other's philosophies, lifestyles, priorities, or ambitions, be like the wind and change direction. Remember that freedom is found only when you control the course of your own life. Now go and plant something that's worthy of your magnificence. You deserve it.

The Call of the Master

Have you seen how profoundly cynical the Impostor has become? The more you see your life from My perspective, the more he fears your rebellion. He knows that your life is a threat to him when you come fully into My heart.

I love this subject of friendship. Perhaps this is why My enemy works so hard to rob My children of the joys that friendships bring. The friends I give you are a gift to grow you and shape you and help you become more like Me. Your friends need you for the same reason. Friendship is the way that you and I and others fellowship together.

Why don't you take some time to meditate on all the people whom I have directed to the door of your heart? See the impact they have had on you since the time you were born? None of them have come into your life by accident. Even those who have caused you pain have been used by Me so I could teach you how to love others the way that I love you.

Now come with Me and let Me use your life to bless the hearts of My people and to lead others to Me. Don't be afraid to keep the doors open. I will not give you more friends than your heart can handle. Join hands with them so that the force of your fellowship will show the world what true friendship looks like. Now trust Me and let Me fill your life with the people of My choosing. Heaven is waiting for the bouquets that will be gathered from within your garden of friends.

The Heart of the Church

I rejoiced with those who said to me,
"Let us go to the house of the LORD."

PSALM 122:1

*H*e entered the building through the back door, making his way quietly through the halls to where the congregation was gathering for morning worship. The sights and sounds of believers assembling beneath the glow of stained-glass windows and an ornately crafted cross caused his nostrils to tingle with inexplicable pleasure. There they all were, dressed in their Sunday best, taking their places in the pews with a smug sense of ownership. Though the building itself was below his expectations, he amused himself with the carryings-on of the people performing almost perfectly for him—their uninvited guest. It was as if they had read the script beforehand and rehearsed the lines for this very occasion. He had to sit on his hands just to keep from clapping. Now was not the time to make a spectacle of himself. No, this was a moment he wanted to drink in and savor. There would be plenty of opportunity to gloat over his victory later, but for now he would sit back and enjoy the morning.

And a sweet victory it was proving to be. Thrown out of heaven kicking and screaming, he swore before God and the poor fools who chose to remain His servants that he would be back. The fact that he was able to sit unnoticed in church with the Master's slaves was all he needed to prove that his craving for revenge was soon to be appeased. He felt a growl erupting from the hollows of his darkened soul. Raising a handkerchief up to his face he managed to hide the traces of saliva dripping from the corners of his lips. He was hungry. *No,* he told himself. *Not yet.* Just a little more time to add the finishing touches on his plan and then the feast could begin. *Hold on…hold on …hold on.*

The Impostor in my church? The very thought is bone-chilling. It's nauseating. Or at least I hope it is. But it's not that far-fetched. It's what he has wanted from the beginning. When he shook his fist in heaven and declared, "I will be like God!" he really believed he could pull it off. After all, up to that point he had only seen the loving side of God. For until then, sin and rebellion had not been an issue in the Master's kingdom.

It must have been humiliating for the beautiful angel to be tossed out of heaven before he had a chance to prove to all the heavenly beings that he was equal to their Creator. It's a grudge he hasn't let go of since he felt the wind against his face as he tumbled down from the celestial city, his voice echoing, "I'll be back!" From that time on, all that he has ever said or done has been driven by his lust to take back the glory that he believes belongs to him.

The Impostor doesn't have to break down the doors of our churches before he can come in and find a place in our pews. All he needs to do is find the weak spots, move into our vulnerable areas; and we will have him in church with us.

TOO MUCH WORLD IN THE CHURCH

Strife in our churches is one area where the Imposter finds a vulnerable place to move into our most sacred arena. I found myself doing battle with the enemy as a war waged in the church I was attending. Independent attitudes were everywhere. So many people wanted their own way that we couldn't find the right way to correct the problem. During that same time period, I had entered the job market. There, in a secular environment, I found more understanding and a stronger sense of cooperation among the *unsaved* employees than we were able to muster within our church body of *sanctified saints*. None of it made sense.

Driving to work along a winding country road one day, I poured out my heart: *Oh, God, why is it that the world seems so much nicer than the church?*

The following year, while driving through that very same bend in the road, God impressed His answer upon my heart. *It's because there is too much world in the church and not enough church in the world.*

A closer look at the church and I knew that God was right. The church had lost its edge. Stories of corruption among the people of God were quickly becoming a nationwide scandal. Magazine articles, TV tabloids, and investigative journalists were having a field day with the men of the cloth whose moral and financial blunders left them exposed to the world's ridicule.

However, underneath the disclosures of embezzlement, fraud, and adultery within Christendom, a greater scandal was brewing. The church was losing its relevance and for the most part, it seemed either too timid to care or too spiteful to turn it around. A few years later during yet another scandal,

I decided to open up the phone lines for discussion with my radio listeners. I began the segment by saying, "When one of our own is caught in adultery, what should be the response of the church?" I gave them three choices. Should we

a) Stone them?
b) Forgive and forget? or
c) Forgive them, ask them to step out of the spotlight, help them get their lives back into alignment with God's heart, and then receive them back into ministry?

To my surprise many callers opted for d) Don't even talk about the subject. Many believed that we shouldn't judge people for their mistakes. When I asked, "How can we talk about sin in the world and then ignore the sin in the church? Can we truly love people if we ignore sin? If we don't ask people to withdraw from public ministry until they have had a good amount of time to get their lives back into alignment with the heart of God, how will we face the world with the gospel of salvation? What will we tell them that they need to be saved from?" The silence that followed my question reminded me of what A. W. Tozer said in his book, *Man, the Dwelling Place of God,* "Complacency is the scandal of Christianity."

The scandal of the church today, I believe, is that we have slipped so easily into the world's culture that we have lost the identification marks of the Master. The church has become a near photocopy of the world with statistics for divorce, promiscuity, infidelity, abortion, alcoholism, and addictions of almost every kind running dangerously close to theirs. As a result, when the consequences of sin crash in on those without God, they have no real place to turn for the answers to life's most critical questions:

- Where can I find forgiveness?
- Where can I find peace?
- Where can I find God?

Finding the weak spots in our lives is how the Impostor goes to church. The weaker we are individually, the weaker we become as a body of believers. The only reason the Impostor wants to go to church with us is to keep these questions from being answered.

WHERE IS THE LIGHT?

The big sins of the church, the ones that show up on the news at night, are only an indication of what is happening within the church as a whole. It is rather an indication that the body as a whole is becoming desensitized to sin. We are losing sight of God's heart for the church. Our complacency seems to say that how we live within the body of Christ doesn't matter to God.

Jesus said that we are the light of the world. But where is that light today? Where is the light of the church that is supposed to be shining in the darkness?

Several years ago, Bud and I served as crewmembers hired to help pilot a yacht from San Diego to La Paz, Mexico. Whenever our turn came to take the midnight watch, we would sit together, holding a hot cup of tea in our hands, and watching the navy blue horizon for the first sign of a passing ship. Inevitably the sign would come. At first a pinpoint of light would peek through the sky like a tiny star resting on the water. Then as the ship neared our boat, the light that had moments before been just a sparkle, lit the ocean around us making the night look almost like day. The game of light spotting kept us awake when our inner time clocks told us we should be sleeping. Finding ships in the dark takes a keen eye and a pressing sense of need—and we needed those lights. One snooze and Danger would be all too eager to plunge us straight to the ocean's floor.

The world can be a very dark place. While we sit around our dinner tables passing the mashed potatoes, we can watch instant replays of the chaos that stalks us daily. Children killing children, tornadoes wiping out whole communities, and leaders explaining away their offensive behaviors have become a steady diet. Political pundits, legal advisors, and psychoanalysts are often called in to give their editorial comments or to explain how and why the lights are going out in our land. But no one has enough wisdom to make sense of it all. No one could.

> Who is like the wise man?
> Who knows the explanation of things?
> Wisdom brightens a man's face
> and changes its hard appearance. (Ecclesiastes 8:1)

A light has been given to lead the world out of its darkness, but we who have been called to carry the light seem to have forgotten how important and powerful that light really is.

Here's another way to put it:

> You're here to be light, bringing out the God-colors
> in the world. God is not a secret to be kept. We're

going public with this, as public as a city on a hill. If I make you light-bearers, you don't think I'm going to hide you under a bucket, do you? I'm putting you on a light stand. Now that I've put you there on a hilltop, on a light stand—shine! (Matthew 5: 14–16, *The Message*)

This is the Master's heart for the church. His offer of eternal life is the greatest news story ever released and made public, that God has chosen a people out of the dark world to be a light for salvation. We are His light that shows the world where they have gone wrong and how to get back to what they were created for. It is this light provided by the church that the Impostor fears most. When the church *behaves* like the church, Satan will be easily spotted slithering through the back door in his snake-skin boots. This is the greatest rebellion of all.

Keeping the light shining in the darkness matters to God.

WHAT *IS* CHURCH?

Pick a church, any church and if it doesn't fit, pick another! Why have we come to the point that we look for a church the way we look for a new pair of shoes? What is church?

The word *church* in America conjures up pictures of grand cathedrals or brick buildings with tall steeples. Yet church is more than a structure where the people of God congregate. It is the Master's *ekklesia* or assembly. We are the heavenly reality of God's redemptive love. It is this gathering together of God's adopted children where prayer, praise, worship, encouragement, teaching, preaching, healing, instruction, correction, equipping, and training in righteousness takes place. It is through this *ekklesia,* that we are called to come together to strengthen each other so we can send each other out into the world to proclaim the message of salvation, then come back together to strengthen each other so we can send each other back out again. It's the M*A*S*H unit for the soldiers of Christ.

Jesus loves the church. Whether it is two at a time or ten thousand He loves to be where His people are gathered together. It has always been in God's heart to build a family where He and they would share His holy love and affection for them, and they would reflect His holiness back to Him. This is what happened in the Garden. Adam and Eve were to become the earthly heads of God's perfect family. But as we have seen, Satan had other plans.

When he tempted Adam and Eve in the Garden, this holy couple of God took on the independence of the Impostor and lost their right to be the head of God's family. But God's plan for a family was not to be thwarted by sin. Instead, He made a promise to man whereby He Himself would bring a people out of mankind who would show the world that He alone is holy and the only requirement from them was that they would be faithful to Him and to His promise.

This promise was first given to Adam. Later, we find God's promise being handed down through Abraham, Moses, and David. The purpose of this Old Testament promise was to choose and keep a people who would be faithful to Him and who would trust His promise to cleanse His people from sin and to make them fit for holy fellowship with Him. Then Jesus came. No longer would the chosen people of God need to trust in the promise to come. The promise was here. Jesus, the Son of God, bearing the same nature as God, died for the sins of all men. The door for fellowship with the holy God was opened. All of us, who have been made holy through the sacrifice of Jesus Christ, can now come into His presence and be His family. We can come together for family gatherings and enjoy the presence of the Head of our family, Jesus. This is church. This is the *ekklesia* of God.

We in the New Testament church now look forward to a new promise. Our hope rests on the coming day when Jesus will return and deal with the Impostor once and for all. He will wipe out all sin, and the world will once again be as it was in the Garden.

> No longer will there be any curse. The throne of God and of the Lamb will be in the city, and his servants will serve him. They will see his face, and his name will be on their foreheads. There will be no more night. They will not need the light of a lamp or the light of the sun, for the Lord God will give them light. And they will reign for ever and ever. (Revelation 22:3–5)
>
> [And Jesus said], "Behold, I am coming soon! Blessed is [she] who keeps the words of the prophecy in this book." (Revelation 22:7)

The church is the Master's living testimony of His unconditional love for mankind. Through the church He lavishes us with His power, wisdom, and never-ending blessings. If the thought of the church doesn't make your heart pound with grateful devotion, maybe you have been looking at the church from the wrong perspective.

How we see church matters to God.

THE CHURCH IS THE BODY OF CHRIST

Just after finishing a lecture for our weekly Bible study, a young woman walked up to me with tears in her eyes. I thought that she must have been moved by my message, so I was prepared to be a loving listener to what was on her heart. However, that sweet moment approaching was not to be. "Sandy," she said, "why is it that you have so many talents, and I have none." If her flattery was meant to be an encouragement to me, it clearly wasn't working.

The memory of her words still makes my heart sad when I think of what they reveal about the recurrent cravings for independence we can often feel within the congregation of believers. *Me, my,* and *mine,* three little words that are a foreign language to the inhabitants of heaven. These possessive pronouns draw us into ourselves, distorting our view of the Master's authority over our lives and the lives of those with whom we have been called to be co-laborers in His kingdom. Seeing what is *ours* and comparing *ours* to what has been given to others leaves us with prideful, bitter, competitive, insecure, and ungrateful hearts. None of us can really know *why* we have been gifted as we have, but each of us is called to know *Who* it is that has given them to us and *how* we are to use them.

Being a member of Christ's body is about more than receiving our fair share of the spiritual blessings that are given to us because we belong to God's household. It is about loving the One who considers us worthy of having them. Our joy in the body of Christ can only be possible when we take our eyes off of ourselves and treasure each member of God's family as if they were the most important members there.

It is like God is saying to us: *I have a dream. And in My*

dream everyone in my house works in harmony with each other. In My dream My people listen to My voice and they use the gifts I give them to bless the lives of others. They love and care for the widows and orphans in their congregation. They teach their children who I am and how to follow My ways. They sing and praise My name. They live holy lives. They go out into the world with My message of eternal life, and they bring new believers into My household of faith. In My dream My children respect their leaders. Older men and women are treated with honor. In My dream My people share not only all their spiritual gifts and worldly possessions, they share their love for Me. They love to gather together because they know that I will be in their midst and will shower My favor upon them.

For God this is more than a dream; it is His will for the church and is the ongoing prayer of His Son. When we understand God's heart for His church, we can't help but fall in love with each member of God's family, for we will see that they are given to spread the glory of Christ everywhere His people are found.

How the body of Christ values each other matters to God.

THE CHURCH IS OUR PRELUDE TO HEAVEN

A prelude can be defined as anything that serves as an introduction or as a preview to a performance. If church is our prelude, or introduction, to heaven, then heaven is just like church.

Now before you decide to sell off your place on the pew, we need to remember that heaven is perfect and we are not. Nevertheless, heaven is the standard for how we should be. Heaven is the pattern for the earthly family of God, and it is the heavenly destination for the people of God. No matter

how much we struggle with getting the pattern straight, we—
the chosen people of God—have nowhere to go but up.

Just as heaven is the pattern for God's earthly family, there
is another pattern set forth in the world for those who follow
the ways of the Impostor. We might say that just as church is
our prelude to heaven, then the world, in all its fleshly independence from God, is a prelude to hell. Two families on one
earth with different fathers, opposite destinations, and very
distinct characteristics—or at least that is how we are supposed to be.

> Dear friend, do not imitate what is evil but what is
> good. Anyone who does what is good is from God.
> Anyone who does what is evil has not seen God. (3
> John 1:11)

God never changes His mind about sin, redemption, and
the way to heaven. He is very clear about who He is, who we
are, and how we can enter into fellowship with Him. There is
no meeting of the minds and no compromises made for those
who think that His word is too divisive. He doesn't want His
people to look like the world.

The world is a melting pot of ideas, values, and behaviors. God has sent His Son into the world to lead us out of the
melting pot and to put us on His path to heaven. He has
come to divide us from the world and to give us a new way
of living. Jesus has come to show us that our way of life is to
be distinctively different than the world's way.

> Your kingdom come, your will be done on earth as it
> is in heaven. (Matthew 6:10)

God's words to me that day on that winding road were perfectly timed to our culture: *There is too much world in the church and not enough church in the world.*

When the world asks us life's most critical questions:

- *Where can I find forgiveness?*
- *Where can I find peace?*
- *Where can I find God?*

What will our living example as a church be?

The holiness of our lives as members of His church matters to God.

THE CHURCH IS OUR FAMILY.

Now here's a statement that can make grown Mommies cry, especially if you have some crazy people in your family.

While I was helping in a VIP booth at Oregon's famous Mt. Hood Jazz Festival one year, the Rainbow Lady stopped by our booth for a cup of cold water. The Rainbow Lady has become a well-loved institution at the festival. She wears a rainbow-colored wig with glitter sprayed on it. Her make-up matches her wig and her clothes match her make-up. I have no idea how the Rainbow Lady came to be or why she dresses the way she does, I only know that she belongs to the festival, and the festival belongs to her. Wherever she goes and whatever she needs, people stop what they're doing to take care of her. Some would say that she is just a crazy lady, but the festival has covered for her and said, "She may be a crazy lady—but she's our crazy lady."

Got any crazy ladies in your church? Well, guess what; they belong to you now. Isn't that how church should be?

The church should be the place that the world looks at and says, "Look at how they all get along. How do they do that?"

We are a family. And as the family of God, we have been called to stick together through thick and thin. This means that we, together, are responsible before God to take responsibility for our own actions and attitudes when faced with the idiosyncrasies of our brothers and sisters in Christ. We need to be forbearing with each other and do all we can to help each other grow up in Christ. When someone in our family is guilty of sin, we need to take God's side of the issue and do all we can to restore them and help them overcome the temptations of the flesh. We will need to set aside our sensitive feelings and allow ourselves to be hurt once in a while without resorting to the revenge of gossip or slander. Above all, we need to agree with God when he says:

> There are six things the LORD hates,
> seven that are detestable to him:
> haughty eyes,
> a lying tongue,
> hands that shed innocent blood,
> a heart that devises wicked schemes,
> feet that are quick to rush into evil,
> a false witness who pours out lies
> and a [woman] who stirs up dissension among [sisters].
> (Proverbs 6:16–19)

How we love each other within the body of Christ matters to God.

THE CHURCH IS THE REPRESENTATION OF THE UNITY OF THE GODHEAD

> I have given them the glory that you gave me, that they may be one as we are one: I in them and you in me. May they be brought to complete unity to let the world know that you sent me and have loved them even as you have loved me. (John 17:22–23)

Don't you just love when you receive a clear and direct answer to prayer? If you're like me, you probably run to the phone so you can spread the news that God answered your prayer. This is the kind of stuff that makes our hearts smile.

A friend of mine called me recently to tell me her good news. A young man that she and her family had spent a year praying for had just asked to be baptized. He had spent a year in defiance toward his family and toward God. Yet, through all the hurt that this young man caused to the people who loved him, the people who loved him continued to pray for him. There were times when he needed to be told that his behavior was wrong. Yet they loved him. There was a time when he needed to be separated from his family and friends. Yet they loved him. Then the day came when he realized that the people who loved him were right about his life. The joy of answered prayer was almost more than all their human hearts could hold.

Every time you and I shower another believer with unconditional love and consider his or her needs above our own, we are an answer to Christ's prayer. Every time we refuse to be a part of gossip, slander, or mistreatment toward a member of Christ's body, we are an answer to His prayer.

Every time we work together with a common desire to bring glory to God through our service in His kingdom, we again are an answer to His prayer.

While the world can write books and hold seminars on how to build happy relationships with other people, the world cannot unite people in one common, holy purpose. The unity of the church proves that God is real and that He alone is able to change each of us completely from what we were into what we were created to be. God is not satisfied to have His children find their own personal happiness individually in Him. He wants us to become one as a body of believers in Him.

Just as Jesus came to separate us from the world, He prayed that we would be made one together in Him. One mind. One heart. One holy body with one common purpose to show the world what God looks like.

> For this reason I kneel before the Father, from whom his whole family in heaven and on earth derives its name. I pray that out of his glorious riches he may strengthen you with power through His Spirit in your inner being, so that Christ my dwell in your hearts through faith. And I pray that you, being rooted and established in love, may have power, together with all the saints, to grasp how wide and long and high and deep is the love of Christ, and to know this love that surpasses knowledge—that you may be filled to the measure of all the fullness of God. (Ephesians 3:14–19)

What would happen if on our way to bed this evening we looked into our room and saw Jesus kneeling by our bed and heard Him praying: "Oh Father, I pray that this dear child will love My church more than she loves herself. I pray that in her thoughts, words, and deeds she will do all things to Your glory as she dwells here on the earth. Give her great joy as she discovers how wonderful it is to belong to this holy family of faith. Guide her steps so that she will know what My purpose for the church really is." Here's the amazing news—we just did. This is His prayer for the body. We can be an answer to His prayer.

The unity of the church matters to God.

THE CHURCH IS THE VEHICLE FOR SALVATION

The new pastor's wife walked into her daughter's Sunday school class and took the teacher aside. The look of seriousness on her face told the teacher that maybe this was going to be a difficult relationship. She was right. The mother explained to the teacher with firm resolve, "If my daughter is told anything about the devil or hell or sin, I will pull her out of this class. These children are far too young to handle this type of teaching." The young teacher looked sincerely into the mother's face and replied, "What can I teach her?" The problem with this particular mother was that she didn't believe in hell. She only believed in heaven. Therefore, she was determined to save her daughter from the discomfort of hearing the story of Jesus' love for sinners.

Hell is not a nice subject. It tends to make people feel bad about themselves. It's sort of like having a doctor say, "Look, I know that you have a knife in your heart, but you're going to be in a lot of pain when I take it out." But hiding from the painful truth doesn't solve our problem with sin.

Jesus knew all about pain. He went up to the Garden of Gethsemane on the Mount of Olives to pray the night before He was arrested. Knowing what He was about to endure as He completed His mission on earth, sweat, which looked like large drops of blood, oozed from His pores. Wanting to escape the suffering that was soon to bring His life to an end, He cried out to His Father, *Save Me, help Me, take this away. But, no…wait…leave Me in it…I will do what is in Your heart for Me to do. Your will is perfect and steady; Mine is encumbered with the frailty of My humanity. Take over…I will do what You require.* An angel came to help Him. Of course. His Father would not have left Him alone without help at this most critical point in history. The pain would be great, but not greater than the reward. He would do it. Salvation was worth the cost.

Salvation is always worth the cost. If we know heaven, we must also grasp the reality of hell; why else would we choose one above the other? J. I. Packer describes the reality of hell in his book *Knowing God* in these words: "The loss, not merely of God, but of all good, and everything that made life seem worth living; 'gnashing of teeth' for self-condemnation and self-loathing."[1]

Unless we face the truth, we, as the church, will not fully accept our mission to bring the message of heaven to those who are destined for hell. We are the vehicles of that message, fueled by grace, and directed by the Holy Spirit to go wherever He leads us. Just as love cannot be left out of the message, we cannot love without the message itself.

For God so loved the world that he gave his one and only Son, that whoever believes in him shall not per-

ish but have eternal life. For God did not send his
Son into the world to condemn the world, but to save
the world through him. (John 3:16–17)

The clear unabridged message of salvation matters to
God.

THE CHURCH IS THE BRIDE OF CHRIST

You want the night to be perfect. You and your husband have
a reservation at the most beautiful restaurant in the world.
Your imagination soars with pictures of glittering chandeliers,
music swirling around the room, starched white tablecloths,
and candles flickering like jewels against the night. You have
carefully planned what you are going to wear. Your hair and
your make-up must be perfect. Nothing can be flawed for this
will be the most memorable evening of your life.

Your expectations are heightened as the clock ticks away
the hours bringing the reality of your evening closer to a cli-
max. Though the room will be beautiful beyond your wildest
dreams, you know that it will be only a backdrop to the
splendor of your loved one's face as you dine together. You
love him so dearly that you feel as if you will die if you miss
the feast. Nothing will keep you from being ready. Pleasing
him is the passion of your heart.

This is the picture of the bride of Christ preparing for the
marriage feast, where she will come to her groom dressed in
white linen. Christ has prepared her garments for her.
Righteous clothing that reflects His character in her will be
the first thing He sees when she walks into the room.

Nothing has been forgotten in the plans for our wedding
feast with the Lamb. Jesus has gone to make the preparations.

But what will the bride do to make herself ready for the Groom?

There was something about being pregnant that threw my ability to bake completely out of whack. I'm still not quite sure what one had to do with the other, but I do know that my family ate much better when I wasn't with child. One day I decided to make my favorite recipe for peanut butter cookies. I measured every ingredient carefully, spooned out my batter on the cookie sheets and when my family walked into the kitchen they inhaled the aroma of their afternoon snack. The cookies looked good. They even tasted somewhat okay. But there was a problem. I had left the peanut butter out of my peanut butter cookies.

There are times when I find myself so busy working in the church, tackling my tasks, and doing all the things that I have committed myself to do, that I forget the main ingredient. The church is the *bride* of Christ. A wedding feast is being prepared for us in heaven. It will be the most magnificent feast in all history. There our groom will receive us as His church. I can't even imagine how perfect that event will be when we as His bride feast with the Lamb in celebration of the fulfillment of His kingdom plan. The battle over the flesh will be over. The Impostor will be destroyed. Sin will be no more. All that we do here on earth we do in preparation for that time when we will stand before our Groom, radiant and full of His glory and reigning with Him as His bride for ever and ever.

> Then I heard what sounded like a great multitude, like the roar of rushing waters and like loud peals of thunder, shouting:

"Hallelujah!
For our Lord God Almighty reigns.
Let us rejoice and be glad
and give him glory!
For the wedding of the Lamb has come,
and his bride has made herself ready.
Fine linen, bright and clean,
was given her to wear."

REVELATION 19:6–8

All my moments here are a preparation for the wedding. I want all of my friends and family to be there. I want my heart to flutter with the excitement of a bride because that is exactly what I am. When the main ingredient is added I find that I have an abundance of joy in everything I do.

Our wedding preparations matter to God.

THE CHURCH IS THE ENEMY OF THE ENEMY

Everything that we have been created for is exactly why the Impostor hates us. He loathes our lives as women, wives, mothers, and friends, and most of all he hates our cooperation together in the Master's household. The last thing he wants us to do is to love the church.

He wants us to love independence the way he does. He wants us to be self-serving and self-focused. He would love for us to be nomadic Christians, dissatisfied with the church and going off on our own to carve out our own ways of being religious.

If we bring our lives into alignment with the heart of the Master, we will become part of a force that is impossible for him to penetrate. When we as women, wives, mothers, workers, and friends join together as a body of believers transformed by the heart of the Master, the power of the Impostor is crushed beneath our feet. It is when we are together, living in loving obedience together, doing what God has given us to do together, serving each other together, worshiping together, growing together, and enduring hardship together, he will be defeated in our lives together.

Building a stronghold against the enemy is important to God.

A TALE OF TWO CHURCHES

When we, the people of God, choose to think in *together* terms, God is able to accomplish the most magnificent things imaginable both in and through us. So why is it that we, the cherished possession of the Master, find church to be such a frustrating issue? Maybe the answer is found in the time we spend sharing our horror stories together. Those ill-fated things that have happened to us because of a few misguided believers playing church without the guidebook, shatter our perspective of how the Master views His church.

There are two stories that illustrate for me what the glory of the church looks like. These are the kinds of stories that cause my heart to say, "Ah, now I get it. Now I see what the Father had in mind when He created the church."

The first one took place just two years ago. The church of which I am privileged to be a member was in the throws of building a building. After years of meeting in school gymnasiums and other church's buildings, we were anxious to complete the project and move in. The cost was enormous. Our budget was like an elephant whose appetite grew bigger every day. No matter how hard we tried to cut corners, new expenses just kept creeping in.

Just when the black numbers were about to turn red, God sent in the troops to help us out. Shortly before Christmas we received an envelope containing a large sum of money from a tiny church in our area. We were stunned. Why had they sent us this? The answer was even more stunning. They did it because they had been praying for us during the entire process. As our pastors relayed the story to our congregation, we wept. The generous little church was too small and the gift was too large, but as always God was not bound to save by many or by few. Joy happens when heaven and earth cry for happiness *together*.

The second story causes a provocative stir in my heart each time I read it. It moves me to consider just how deep my love for the body of Christ actually goes. It happened in Rwanda during the massacre that took the lives of hundreds of thousands of people in just a matter of days. The loss was so great that it was hard to comprehend the numbers in terms of individuals. Carl Lawrence in his book *Rwanda, A Walk through Darkness into Light* helped me to see this murderous spectacle from God's perspective. I haven't been the same since.

> More than two hundred people sought sanctuary in a local church. The Hutu militia came and called them outside. As they gathered men, women, and children, the militia leader told all the Hutus to separate themselves from the Tutsis and to step to one side. Everyone knew what would happen; as soon as this was done there would be the staccato of AK-47s, the blast of hand grenades, the glare of striking machetes, after which the Hutus would be free to return to the sanctuary.

As if each of them were instructed by an inner voice, all of them, Hutus and Tutsis, moved as one to the side. The militia became frustrated and told them they misunderstood, Hutus were to separate themselves. Again the order was given. "All Tutsis move back to where you were, and Hutus, stay where you are." Again, all moved as one.

The cursing of the militia leader was silenced by the pastor, himself a Hutu. He stepped forward and without animosity quietly told the militia leader, "We are neither Hutu nor Tutsi. We are Christian. We are all brothers in the Lord Jesus Christ."

A holy silence was shattered by the sound of hot metal piercing the innocent bodies of men, women, and children, followed by the hacking sounds of glittering pieces of metal against non-resistant human flesh. And then silence again. The church had been given a powerful, and final, message.[2]

The Call of the Imposter

Here is exactly what I've been trying to protect you from. This is why I have been calling you to come away and find your freedom in me. I know what it feels like to be rejected by this heavenly order of things. Believe me when I tell you that if you lose your independence, you lose everything that you have been created for.

The choice is really very clear. Either you want to be joined at the hip with a group of people you don't really know or you want the freedom to love those whom you choose to love. Which will it be? I know you might be afraid to strike out on your own, but look at me. I have never regretted my flight out of heaven. You are a part of creation's glory. Nothing you do can change that. Yet there are those who want to stifle your growth and keep you from knowing the truth about your freedom.

There is a new day dawning in this thing called church. My people are gaining in numbers and we are getting ready to take back what belongs to us. The church does not belong to a select few; it belongs to all of us. Soon we will march through its doors and liberate it from its bondage to the Master. When that is accomplished none of us will have any need of a leader. We will find our glorious sovereignty in ourselves and worship it together. Now come and let us take our place on the pew.

The Call of the Master

I have chosen from the beginning to create a world and to fashion a people who would know Me and share in My eternal glory. My glory is Mine, and I will never share it with another. That is why I have called you to come out of the darkness of the world and to come into the light of My kingdom.

I have invited you to come into My heart and to see My church. It's not a building or a special denomination of believers. It is a living body that is designed to be My light to those who will perish without it.

All that you are and all that you do matters greatly to Me. You are not your own. You were designed with a purpose. I have created you to be a part of My forever family, so I want you to live in such a way that you bear the resemblance of Me wherever you go and in whatever you do. I love My family, the church, and I have called the church, of which you are a member, to reveal My heart to the world. So love Me and love My church. Resist the impulses of your flesh to grow weary in doing good to those with whom you have been joined together. I made you for each other, and one day you will see why your unity is so important to Me.

Every day that you live is a gift from Me. Use my gift as a means of preparing yourself and my kingdom for the time when all the deeds of My enemy will be exposed, and he will be cast into total darkness forever. Look forward with Me to the time when the celebration of the wedding feast will take place. There you, My perfect and holy bride, will be given the honor to feast at My table, with all those who through all time have chosen Me.

*Come and Join
the Rebellion!*

*H*ow many women will it take to launch a rebellion? It can begin with just you and me. Together we can make a distinctive difference in our homes, in our churches, and in the world. The good news is that the tide is already turning. Women who are tired of living under the lies of the Impostor are heeding the call to come home to the heart of the Master.

In 1997, I had the privilege of going to Pasadena, California, to work with Chosen Women, a national women's conference committed to preparing God's women for revival. On Saturday afternoon, I went down onto the field in front of the stage to help the media find the best places to set up equipment. There I listened as Susan Kimes, the founder of Chosen Women, gave a stirring message about what it means to surrender our hearts and lives to Jesus Christ.

When Susan came out on stage, she was wearing a black raincoat with big rubber boots. A dark hat nearly covered her face, and she was carrying a large black umbrella. I took one look at her and felt a little homesick for the wet weather in Oregon. Then as Susan began her message, she explained how her clothing was an illustration of how our hearts have become covered by the world's ways. As best as I can remember, the hat represented the world's philosophies that keep us from understanding God's Word. The umbrella was a barrier to the Holy Spirit's power. The raincoat was the burdens of the world being carried on our shoulders, and the boots were the feet that are traveling down the wrong path. As each of these items was removed, you really had the feeling of the freedom that is ours when we surrender ourselves completely to Christ.

Then Susan gave a most unusual challenge to the women in the grandstands. Her call to action went something like this.

"Ladies, from where you are sitting, I want you to find a white flag of surrender. It can be a handkerchief, a sweater, a tissue, or just a white piece of paper. While you consider what things you have been holding on to, I'm going to ask the choir to lead us as we sing, 'I Surrender All.' Then as you are singing, I want those of you who have been holding on to things that God never intended for you to carry, to release them to Jesus. As you give your burdens to Him, I want you to wave your white flags of surrender."

Thousands of women sat in their seats waving their white flags. The revolution had begun. I had just gone through a point of discouragement in the process of writing this book. But when I saw all those women waving their flags in tearful surrender, my heart too was overcome with emotion. *Oh, God, this book is not just another goal that I want to achieve. This is Your heart unfolding before Your women. You are moving in us to bring us back to You in full and complete submission.* I waved my white flag.

I believe that God is calling us today to become rebels for His sake. He is seeking the hearts of women who are willing to take a stand against the lies of the Impostor. Will you be one who will say yes to the Master's call? Will you be one who will dare to stand before the enemy of God in the power of God and take a stand for God? I'm asking you, as we come to the end of this book, to put your right hand out against the Impostor and take a stand with me in saying, "No more."

No more will we as God's chosen women allow our lives to be deceived by a false ruler whose true intention is to destroy the kingdom of the Master.

No more will we share our affection for the God who loves us with unwavering grace, compassion, forgiveness, and has lavished us with blessings too numerous to count, with the Impostor.

No more will we give our time to the Impostor and resist the Master's voice as He calls us daily to come and sit at His feet to learn from Him, commune with Him, and receive direction for our steps.

No more will we dishonor our husbands by failing to love them with reverent hearts and submissive spirits. Instead, we will entrust ourselves to the Master who will help us to become one in the same way as He has become one with us.

No more will we deny the profound importance of our homes. Instead, we dedicate our homes to the ways of the Master so that our earthly dwellings will reflect the unity, joy, praise, and order of our heavenly homes.

No more will we listen to the lies of the Impostor regarding the value of motherhood. We will love being our children's mothers, and we will gladly sacrifice what is needed to help our children discover the Master's will for their lives. We will submit ourselves to the design of our Creator and surrender to the joy that motherhood is intended to be.

No more will we find our worth in our briefcases. We will allow the Master to choose our career paths for us, and we will dedicate ourselves to be kingdom servers wherever He commissions us to go. We will no longer search on our own for significance, but we will let Christ determine how best to meet our needs for joy and fulfillment.

No more will we be consumed by the Impostor's vanity. We will seek instead to be bearers of the Master's beauty. We will not fear growing older, but we will look to the Master to perfect His beautiful image in us. We will stay away from the Impostor's closet. We will only wear the Master's righteous clothing so that our character and our deeds will prove who, as well as Whose, we are.

No more will we allow friendship to be an escape from our life's priorities. We will see our friends as instruments of the Master to grow and shape us to be more like Him. When we get hurt we will not shrink back or close the door to friendship. Instead, we will fling wide the gates of our hearts and let the people of His choosing come in.

No more will we abandon our love for the church because the people in it have disappointed us. We will strengthen the church by our commitment to grow to maturity and minister the same love and compassion to its members that Christ ministers to us. We together will be the Master's light shining in the darkness leading others to where eternal life is found. We will proclaim to the world that our citizenship is in heaven, and our church will reflect our true identity.

Our hearts matter to God. How we love Him matters to God. What we do as His women matters to God. How we treat our families matters to God. How we treat our friends matters to God. How we love His church matters to God. Everything about us matters to God.

For the eyes of the Lord range throughout the earth
to strengthen those whose hearts are fully committed
to him. (2 Chronicles 16:9a)

Two calls have been given at the end of each of the chapters throughout this book. Because we have no written transcript of the Impostor, we can only imagine how he would speak to us as the chosen women of God. Yet we do know the Master. His Word has been given to us; He has not hidden His will or His ways from us. Everything about Him has been fully disclosed. Would you follow the one who hides in the shadow, or the real thing? Now is the time to make your decision as to whose call you will choose to answer.

On the final two pages you will find two living wills. I am trusting that you would not be so foolish, after everything that you have read, to choose to follow anyone other than the Master Himself. Therefore, these two living wills are written so that you might declare in writing your decision from this time forward to join with those of us who have already said *yes* to the Master and *no* to the Impostor. Read them through very carefully, and then prayerfully sign them. Keep them near you so that when you are tempted to forget the decision you have made, you can go back to your living will and remember to whom you belong.

If you never go against the grain you will never make anything smooth.

If you never stand out in a crowd you will never know your true identity.

If you don't stand up for what is right, you will never know what's wrong with being wrong.

The Master is calling to you and to me and to all who have His heart in us to choose this day whom we will serve and to heed the call of rebellion.

My Living Will

I know you! You are the great Impostor. Will your lies never end? I have been seeing people the way you see them, as a means of self-gain. Your view of life is egotistical and self-serving. Your desire for the church is straight from the pit of hell. You have tried in every way to turn my attention toward myself so that I will be rendered useless in the Master's kingdom. You don't really want *me* do you? You want to destroy the bride of Christ. That has been your plan all along.

Now that I know who you are and what you are about, I hereby bequeath,

Nothing

By the power of the Living God, I give my living will to the One who has won my heart—your Enemy, the Master. My identity is in Him, my allegiance is to Him, my affection is for Him, my service belongs to Him, and my destination is heaven where I will live with Him forever. I will never be yours. I take this stand of rebellion against you with confidence because I know who my Master is, and I testify to you today, in the presence of the Master's kingdom, that I will follow your Enemy forever.

Signed_____

in the presence of God on this date:_____

My Living Will

I know You. You are my Master. You have patiently loved me while I have been listening to the lies of Your enemy. Yet You have not abandoned me while I have foolishly followed my flesh, the empty ways of the world, and even the Impostor himself.

Your great love has won me over in every area of my life. I am fully Yours. Though You know the battle for my heart will continue to rage, nevertheless, I know that You have already won the war through the power of Your resurrection. I am Yours.

Therefore, I bequeath to You today, all of who I am. I purpose from this day forward to see every aspect of my life from Your perspective. I submit my living will to You and confess that You alone are the LORD of all that concerns me. My identity, my loved ones, the world, and the church all belong to You. I trust You to fill my heart with Your incomparable riches, wisdom, power, grace, mercy, holiness, and love. To You, my only Master, from this moment forth I declare that everything You desire for me is, "Yes, and Amen."

Signed_____

in the presence of God on this date:_____

BIBLIOGRAPHY/READING LIST
IF YOU WANT TO BE A REBEL, BE A READER

Reading has been the backbone of my growth in Christ. I invite you into my library to discover more about what it means to live a single-hearted love for Christ.

CHAPTER ONE: THE CHOSEN HEART

Myrna Alexander, *Behold Your God* (Grand Rapids, Mich: Zondervan Publishers, 1982).

Henry Blackaby and Claude V. King, *Experiencing God* (Nashville, Tenn.: Broadman & Holman, 1993).

John Piper, *Desiring God* (Sisters, Ore.: Multnomah Publishers, Inc., 1996).

John Piper, *Future Grace* (Sisters, Ore.: Multnomah Publishers, Inc., 1995).

John Piper, *Godward Life* (Sisters, Ore.: Multnomah Publishers, Inc., 1997).

CHAPTER TWO: ONE HEART, ONE MASTER

Kay Arthur, *Lord, I'm Torn Between Two Masters* (Sisters, Ore.: Multnomah Publishers, Inc., 1996).

Rebecca Manley Pippert, *A Heart Like His* (Wheaton, Ill. Crossway Books, 1996).

Jeanne Hendricks, *Women of Honor* (Sisters, Ore.: Multnomah Publishers, Inc., 1995).

CHAPTER THREE: A HEART IN TRAINING

Richard Foster, *Celebration of Discipline* (San Francisco: Harper SanFrancisco, 1988).

Ruth Myers, *31 Days of Praise* (Sisters, Ore.: Multnomah Publishers, Inc., 1998).

Charles Haddon Spurgeon, *Morning by Morning* (Downwood, Claverton Down Road, Bath BA 26DT, Creative Publishing, 1985).

CHAPTER FOUR: THE HEART THAT SAYS, "I DO"

Bunny Wilson, *Liberated through Submission* (Eugene, Ore.: Harvest House Publishers, 1997).

Frank and Bunny Wilson, *The Master's Degree* (Eugene, Ore.: Harvest House Publishers, 1996).

Denalyn Lucado, *The Joy of a Promise Kept* (Sisters, Ore.: Multnomah Publishers, Inc., 1998).

CHAPTER FIVE: THE HOMEWARD HEART

Carol Brazo, *No Ordinary Home* (Sisters, Ore.: Multnomah Publishers, Inc., 1995).

Alice Gray, *Stories for the Family's Heart* (Sisters, Ore.: Multnomah Publishers, Inc., 1998).

Nancy Kennedy, *Help I'm Being Intimidated by the Proverbs 31 Woman* (Sisters, Ore.: Multnomah Publishers, Inc., 1995).

CHAPTER SIX: A NEW HEART FOR MOM

Dr. David Walls, *Parenting By the Book* (Gresham, Ore.: Vision House Publishing, Inc.).

Robin Jones Gunn, *Mothering by Heart* (Sisters, Ore.: Multnomah Publishers, Inc.).

Nancy Kennedy, *Mom on the Run* (Sisters, Ore.: Multnomah Publishers, Inc., 1996).

CHAPTER SEVEN: THE HEART IN A BRIEFCASE

Judith Couchman, *Designing a Woman's Life* (Sisters, Ore.: Multnomah Publishers, Inc., 1998).

Mary Farrar, *Choices—For Women Who Long to Discover Life's Best* (Sisters, Ore.: Multnomah Publishers, Inc., 1997).

Brenda Hunter, *Home By Choice* (Sisters, Ore.: Multnomah Publishers, Inc., 1993).

CHAPTER EIGHT: THE BEAUTIFUL HEART OF A REBEL

Alice Gray, *Stories for a Woman's Heart* (Sisters, Ore.: Multnomah Publishers, Inc., 1999).

Sandra Simpson LeSourd, *The Not-So Compulsive Woman* (Tarrytown, N.Y.: Chosen Books, 1992).

Sheri Rose Shepherd, *Fit for Excellence* (Orlando, Fl.: Creation House, 1992).

CHAPTER NINE: THE HEART OF FRIENDSHIP

Brenda Hunter, *In the Company of Friends* (Sisters, Ore.: Multnomah Publishers, Inc., 1996).

Lucibel Van Atta, *Women Encouraging Women* (Sisters, Ore.: Multnomah Publishers, Inc., 1988).

CHAPTER TEN: THE HEART OF THE CHURCH

Charles W. Colson, *The Body* (Dallas, Tex.: Word Publishers 1992).

Ken Hutcherson, *The Church* (Sisters, Ore.: Multnomah Publishers, Inc., 1998).

Tom Phillips, *Revival Signs—Join the Coming New Spiritual Awakening* (Sisters, Ore.: Multnomah Publishers, Inc., 1995).

NOTES

CHAPTER ONE

1. Dr. Neil Andersen, adapted from *Released from Bondage* (Here's Life Publishers, Inc., 1991), 241–42.

2. Charles Haddon Spurgeon, *Morning by Morning* (Downwood, Claverton Down Road, Bath BA 26DT, Creative Publishing, 1985), 28.

CHAPTER TWO

1. Joseph Bayly, *Psalms of My Life* (Colorado Springs, CO., ChariotVictor Publishing).

CHAPTER THREE

1. John Piper, *Future Grace* (Sisters, Ore.: Multnomah Publishers, Inc., 1995), 26.

2. Oswald Chambers, *My Utmost for His Highest,* updated edition (Grand Rapids, Mich.: Chambers Publications Association Ltd., 1992), 15.

3. Richard Foster, *Celebration of Discipline* (San Francisco: Harper San Francisco), 17.

CHAPTER SIX

1. Wayne Barber, *The Rest of Grace* (Eugene, Ore.: Harvest House Publishers, 1998), 37.

CHAPTER TEN

1. J. I. Packer, *Knowing God* (Downers Grove, Ill.: InterVarsity Press, 1973), 153.

2. Carl Lawrence, *Rwanda: A Walk through Darkness into Light* (Sisters, Ore.: Multnomah Publishers, Inc.), 139–40.